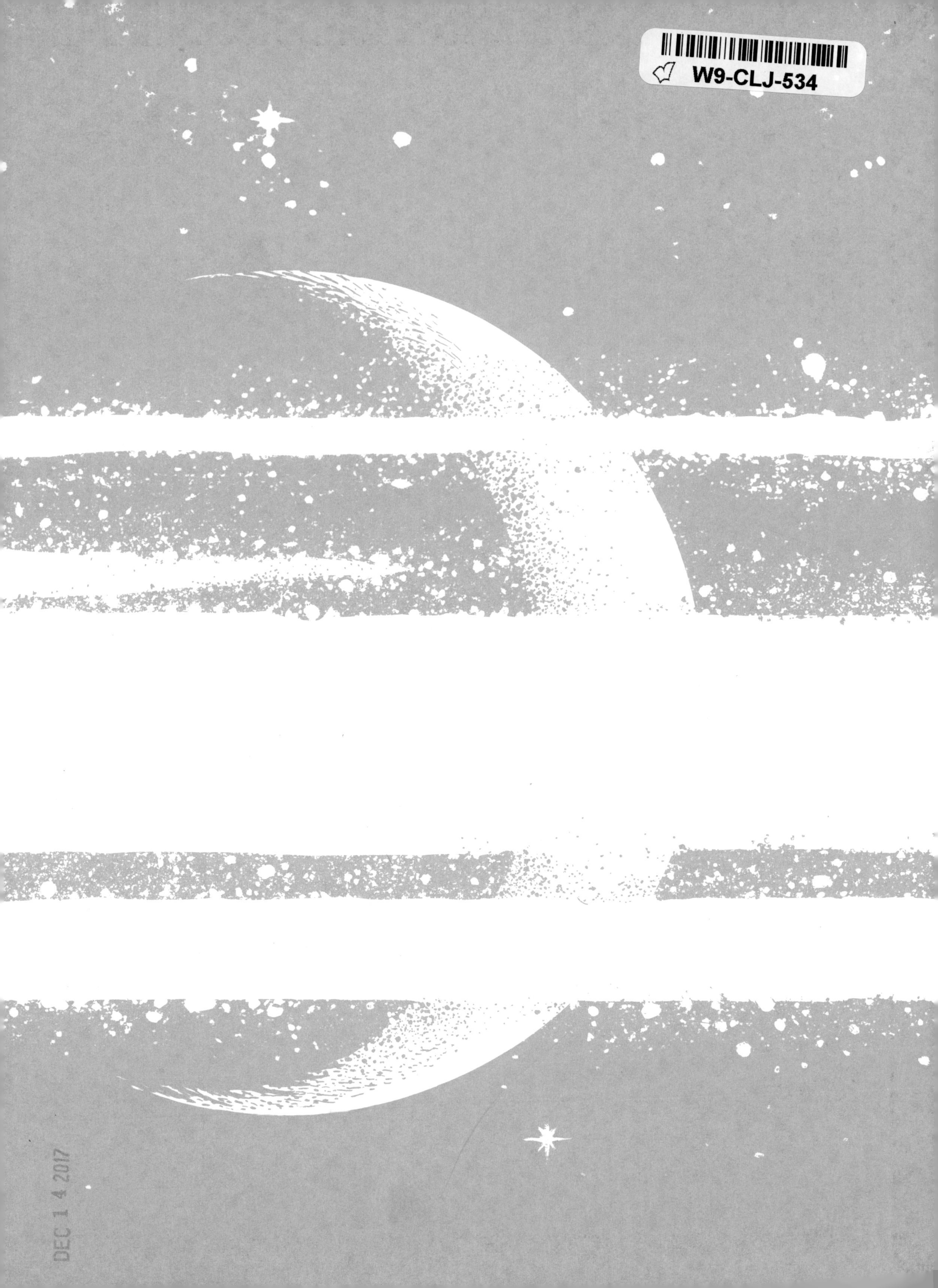

CHRISTIN   MÉZIÈRES

VALERIAN

THE COMPLETE COLLECTION VOLUME 2

9th CINEBOOK
The 9th Art Publisher

VALERIAN

THE COMPLETE COLLECTION VOLUME 2

SCRIPT **PIERRE CHRISTIN**   ARTWORK **JEAN-CLAUDE MÉZIÈRES**

COLOURS ÉVELYNE TRANLÉ

9th CINEBOOK
The 9th Art Publisher

Original title: Valerian – L'Intégrale Volume 2
Original edition: © Dargaud Paris, 2016 by Christin, Mezières & Tranlé
www.dargaud.com
All rights reserved
English translation: © 2016 Cinebook Ltd
Translator: Jerome Saincantin
Lettering and text layout: Design Amorandi
This edition first published in Great Britain in 2017 by
Cinebook Ltd
56 Beech Avenue
Canterbury, Kent
CT4 7TA
www.cinebook.com
Second printing: June 2017
Printed in Spain by EGEDSA
A CIP catalogue record for this book
is available from the British Library
ISBN 978-1-84918-356-7

9th CINEBOOK
The 9th Art Publisher

INTERVIEW LUC BESSON, JEAN-CLAUDE MÉZIÈRES AND PIERRE CHRISTIN (PART 2)

BY CHRISTOPHE QUILLIEN

IN THE SECOND PART OF THIS EXCLUSIVE AND PREVIOUSLY UNPUBLISHED INTERVIEW WITH LUC BESSON, JEAN-CLAUDE MÉZIÈRES AND PIERRE CHRISTIN, READERS WILL DISCOVER THAT BRINGING A VALERIAN AND LAURELINE ADVENTURE INTO EXISTENCE IS NO WALK IN THE PARK. THE AUTHOR ('I CAN'T BELIEVE YOU EDITED MY TEXT!') AND THE ARTIST ('IT WAS TOO LONG!') SPEND MOST OF THEIR TIME SQUABBLING AMIABLY DURING THE CREATION OF A BOOK. AS FOR THE DIRECTOR OF THE FILM ADAPTED FROM THEIR STORIES, HE TURNS INTO A KIND OF WAR BOSS IN COMMAND OF 900 PEOPLE.

Jean-Claude Mézières, Luc Besson and Pierre Christin.

© Virginie Besson-Silla

Luc Besson, how are you going to appeal to a new audience that don't know *Valerian* and make them love the comic series?

Luc Besson: In order to appeal to viewers, you absolutely shouldn't try to please them! That's a straight path to failure. If there were sure-fire approaches, everyone would adopt them and every film would be a success. The important thing is to express yourself as you are; to be honest and confident; to go all the way while telling yourself that, touch wood, there'll always be people who think the same way and love the same things you do. Those who think they can make it by copying a successful film are wrong. Right after I made *Nikita*, we were subjected to a wave of sub-*Nikitas*...

As for me, I try to make films that I'd like to see in a cinema. When *Lucy* became a hit, for example, it took everyone by surprise. It hadn't made the lists of the year's most expected films, or even the summer blockbusters lists. *Lucy* came out of nowhere, and it was its freshness that made the difference. Everybody always wonders why a film didn't work, but we should also wonder why another did find its audience. I'm working along the same lines with *Valerian*: the aim is to offer something different.

Pierre Christin: This approach is coherent with the way we've envisioned *Valerian* ever since the beginning of the series.

We've often been asked if this was a comic for children or adults, but the truth is that we've never asked ourselves that question! You can read *Valerian* when you're in your teens and then read it five years later with completely new eyes. Success can also be a question of circumstances. Sometimes a volume will capture something of the spirit of the times without the authors really trying to. That's what happened to us when we tackled gender relations, for example. The only merit of *Valerian* and its creators is to have always shied away from stereotypes.

Do a film and a comic series have the same longevity?

Jean-Claude Mézières: At first *Valerian* books had slow, steady sales figures. While we did receive a rather favourable welcome when we started out, there was never a rush of readers. We had time to introduce them to the series gradually. The pressure is completely different in cinema: a film only has a week or two to make its mark.

Luc Besson: That's right - but then again, that's wrong too. It's true that you can see that rush effect in the week that follows the cinematic release - as if you could already call it a success or failure by 2 p.m. on the first day. But a film's life goes well beyond that nowadays. A film that makes an impression will be traded between friends, gifted between parents and children, shown on TV regularly. As I grow older, I feel the excitement of release day less and less. A film that gets off to a bad start can still score big in the long term. I had an amusing experience in Asia a few months ago. A thirteen-year-old Korean boy with a red Mohican ran up and told me, '*Subway* is my favourite movie!' He wasn't even born when *Subway* came out, but maybe he fell in love with the film because it takes place in the Paris Métro and shows characters that are very exotic to his eyes...

Pierre Christin: The great strength of comics is the collector who owns every single volume of the series and takes loving care of them. I even know a few who bought two copies of each *Valerian*. One is for their private library and no one's allowed to touch it. The other they allow their children to read... Forty years after they were published, those books remain revered objects. There was a time when the 'art-house' cinema circuit fulfilled the same role for films. A small group of enthusiasts kept the memory of films alive, but the collective memory of cinema was much weaker. Today it's far stronger. Films have a longer life, thanks to media such as DVDs.

Luc Besson: I recently found a load of '70s *Pilote* issues, in which *Valerian* was published. It felt strange - for the first time in ages I was looking at covers that I'd quite forgotten, but that I'd spent hours staring at when I was a teenager... It'd be great if the film could make as strong and long-lasting an impression on its viewers!

There's no villain in *Valerian*. Is that a handicap for a modern science-fiction film?

Luc Besson: You'll meet some bad guys, of course, but they're not quite the caricatures you see in most films. They're not out to destroy the Earth, and that's what makes them interesting. I find villains fascinating. In my films I like to show that the good guys aren't necessarily nice, and the bad guys aren't always who we think they are... In *Leon - The Professional*, the chief of police is an absolute scumbag, while the contract killer isn't all that bad. He's an assassin, yeah, and guilty, but he does rescue a little girl, whereas the police fail to do so. I enjoy this uncertainty. In real life, arms dealers often go to church on Sundays and put money in the poor box; people like them because they have a reputation for generosity. But that doesn't stop them from manufacturing anti-personnel mines or chemical weapons.

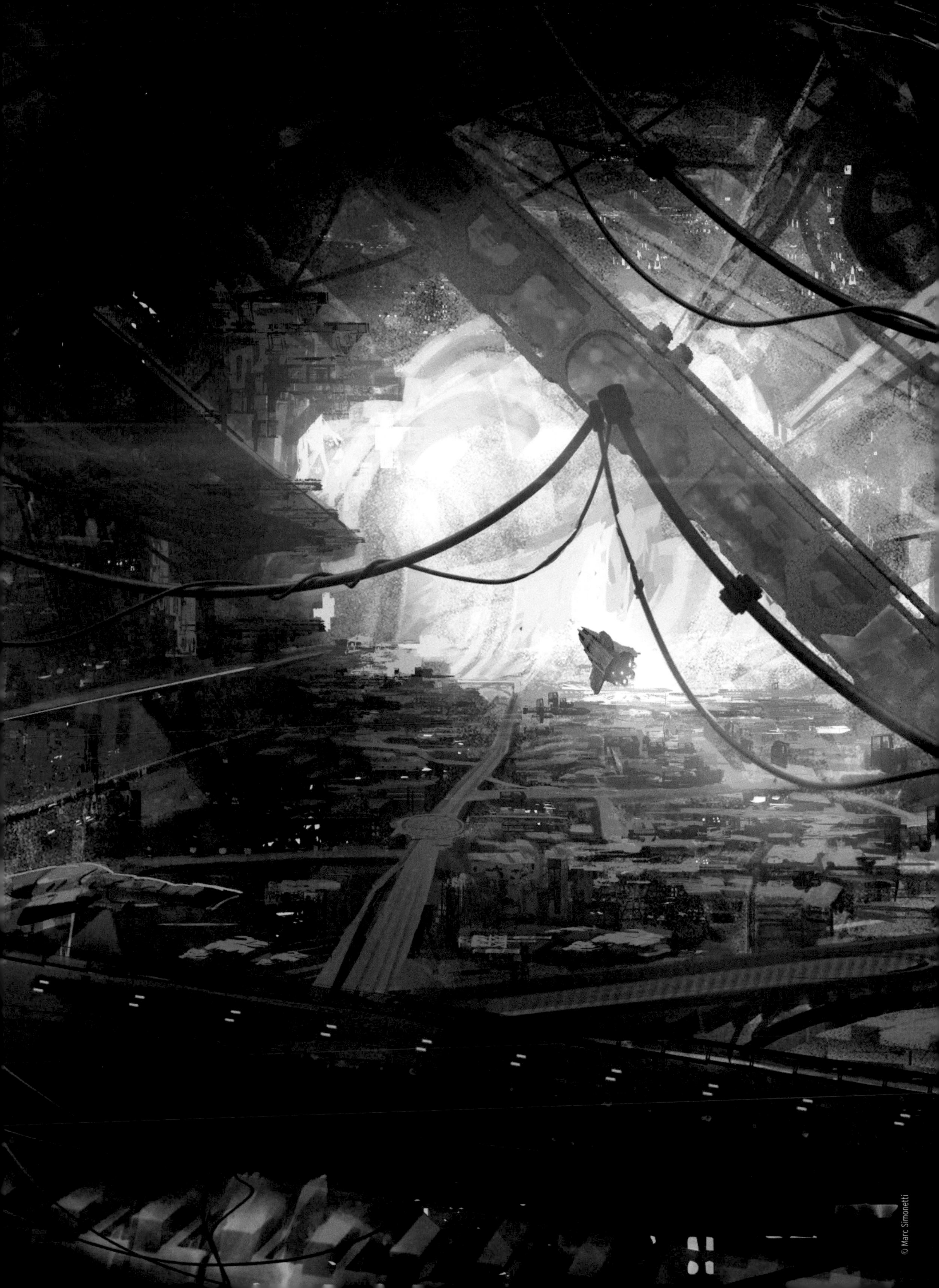

Jean-Claude Mézières: You know the usual argument: 'That may be so, but they still provide work for people...'

Luc Besson: Yes, that's generally the answer you get. Meanwhile, the dishevelled grumpy guy who's always griping about something will be labelled a pain in the neck... Therein lies all the ambiguity of life and our society. I prefer to touch upon this theme in my movies, rather than show a superhero saving us from the supervillain on to whom we project all our fears and worries.

Pierre Christin and Jean-Claude Mézières, was it your intention to use this ambiguity when you created *Valerian*?

Pierre Christin: It was our intention. Take the theme of environmentalism, for example. Back then, it didn't exist politically and the word was rarely used. The book *Welcome to Alflolol* illustrates this ambiguity. It's tempting for readers to label the Terrans who exploit planet Alflolol as 'evil' and the Alflololians as 'good' – simple people who live with almost nothing. But on the other hand, the machine must keep going. Those who damage a world – and damage themselves doing so – are also doing something useful. I remember that the 'greens' at the time reproached us for being too soft on industrialists...

Luc Besson: I always found the political side of that story very interesting. The Alflololians go off on a bit of a walkabout through space for a few thousand years. And when they come back, they find a load of squatters – the Humans – plundering their world... I think it's quite understandable that they tell the interlopers, 'Hey, you lot, we don't mean to be rude but this is our home!'

Pierre Christin: The Humans didn't have bad intentions...

Luc Besson: True, they didn't know they were on an inhabited planet.

Luc Besson, at what stage of the adaptation do you come in?

Luc Besson: First of all, writing the script. That's the most creative and most exciting part of the process: I'm all alone and I'm not bothering anyone! It's at that stage that I feel the most in tune with Christin and Mézières. Afterwards I change my hat and turn into a director – and become a veritable general! I'm not the same man: I must make a decision every 4 seconds, I'm facing 2,700 shots over 23 weeks of shooting, and I command a team of 900... It's not the part I like best, but it's still very stimulating. You see the film being born right before your eyes; you do costume tests, you start working with the actors... Those are very enjoyable moments that bring a lot of pleasure.

Do you keep reading the series at every stage of the creation?

Luc Besson: While writing the script, I take the time to reread the books and savour them over a cup of tea... But during filming I have a real job to do. I like to compare shooting a film to mining coal – relatively speaking. First you have to extract the raw material, which is a kind of rough diamond that we'll have to cut and polish during shooting.

Everything that comes afterwards – recording the score, designing the poster, making the trailer – is like a shiny present with a nice ribbon around it. The shooting really is the tough part of film making, with strict schedules to follow, weather constraints, actors that get sick or miss

a plane... It's an exhausting machine and a very physical stage.

Pierre Christin, does a *bande dessinée* scriptwriter get the same pleasure?

Pierre Christin: My feelings are similar, but my constraints aren't the same. A comic writer sits comfortably before their computer screen... There is one extraordinary moment: when I discover the pages that Jean-Claude has drawn. A script is nothing but a load of paper and not a very enjoyable read, apart from the dialogue bits. It's more of a technical document, a kind of sales pitch that's supposed to explain what needs to be done for the story to hold together. When I see the panels and the pages, what had been sort of bundled together in a corner of my mind springs to life before my eyes. That's amazing!

Luc Besson: Pierre, do you ever have to rework your dialogue because of speech-bubble size?

Pierre Christin: Usually Jean-Claude won't hesitate to chop off some of my text, supposedly because it won't fit inside a bubble... Our discussions can get tense! 'Look at that, it's ugly – it's spoiling my art!' he tells me with a straight face, speaking about the lines of dialogue he finds too long. And I answer, 'Maybe. But maybe you haven't noticed that the text says something important about the story!' I'd say a good fourth of my excellent dialogue has been pruned along the way...

Jean-Claude Mézières: And what about my excellent art, huh? You can always write shorter sentences...

Pierre Christin: He makes the text run out of the panel on purpose so he can tell me, 'See? I told you it wouldn't fit.' He's just out to annoy me!

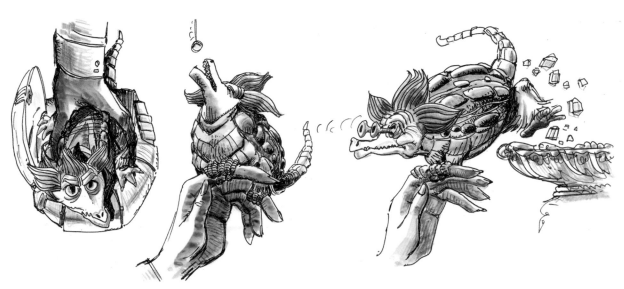

Studies by J.C. Mézières for the film.

Is it necessary to keep some distance from a story when you're adapting it for the big screen?

Luc Besson: The book is like the foundations of a house. It allows me to anchor myself in something solid that helps me move forward. Later, like an architect, I can change such and such element to account for wind or sun exposure, but I'm still building on foundations and three or four concrete pillars.

And is the author worried about seeing his universe turned upside down?

Pierre Christin: No, I'm not worried at all. On the contrary. A comic book doesn't really elicit an emotional response, apart from the beauty of the art and colours. It suffers from a lack of inner dimension. You could say that we know what goes on in Snowy's head better than in Tintin's! Readers see the characters act and talk, but it's very difficult for them to delve inside their inner world. On the other hand, with cinema, the audience has the good fortune of seeing actors on screen, and that creates a sort of empathy with them. It spontaneously generates emotion. Moreover, cinema also uses sound effects and music – two tools that comics don't have access to.

Luc Besson: Speaking of sound, in the comic, Valerian and Laureline's ship makes none. So it was up to us to imagine it – that's the job of the sound designers. They come in with some thirty sounds, and we listen to them one by one before choosing several snippets to arrive at the one that's most suitable.

What are the technical limits to a film like Valerian?

Luc Besson: There aren't any – nowadays, imagination is the only limit in film-making. The technology allows us to do anything and everything. We could show someone yawning and a whale coming out of their mouth if we wanted to! Actually, I'm convinced that France and Europe as a whole have a key role to play in this sector. When you look closely at the history of French culture, you clearly see how incredibly rich it is in all areas, from painting to architecture. It's the only way to close the economic gap with the United States and its 300 million inhabitants – especially as we're seeing a decline in the content quality of American adventure and science-fiction films.

The interview will be concluded in volume 3 of Valerian: The Complete Collection.

Above: *Dane DeHaan as Valerian.*
The illustrations accompanying this interview are studies made by the film's team, based on the work of Jean-Claude Mézières.

THE INTERGALACTIC UNITES THE HUMAN RACE!

BY STAN BARETS

'A MAN WITH A SOUL OBEYS ONLY THE UNIVERSE.'
EPICTETUS

If Mézières is the master of images, then Christin is the virtuoso wordsmith. He's also the ideologist of the pair. Anyone curious about his appearance will find his caricature in *Orphan of the Stars* (see page 14 of this book). Mézières placed him there, glasses perched atop his head, playing the tailor-made role of a storyteller. And the author, who began his career under the pen name of Linus, mischievously puts this question in the mouth of his two-dimensional double: 'What's the point of a scriptwriter?' The artist answers, 'He feeds the story, gives it a narrative structure, provides our paper actors with dialogues.'

DR. CHRISTIN...

When you ask Christin to define himself, his answer is simple: 'By education I'm a typical French intellectual, influenced by Marxism and the analysis of power struggles. Politically speaking, I'm a hard-line reformist.' Born in 1938, he attended the Paris Institute of Political Studies and the University of Paris-Sorbonne, where he obtained a PhD – with a thesis on 'Man-bites-dog journalism – the poor man's literature'. Sent to teach at the University of Bordeaux, in 1968 he created its school of journalism, which he ran for many years and contributed to for many more. In a lot of ways, Pierre Christin is a very serious gentleman with his feet firmly on the ground.

...AND MR LINUS.

And yet, when you get to know him, the man is more a doubter than a doctor. His feet may be on the ground, but his head seems far above the clouds! In the '60s a jumble of things captured his interest: the American way of life, jazz, popular cinema, noir novels and black music ... and, above all, science fiction.

Being an intellectual, he devoured that literature first in *Fiction* and *Galaxie*, essential purveyors of translated material at the time, before moving on to reading it in the original language. When asked to quote influential names, they come gushing out: 'Back then it was Wyndham, Van Vogt, Asimov, Anderson. Later came Jack Vance, the cyberpunks or Dan Simmons.' This man carries several libraries in his head: 'What really matters is the world of imagination,' he says. So it is little wonder that he had the urge to write very early. And, in truth, the author of *Valerian* shouldn't eclipse the writer.

With *Le Futur est en marche arrière (The Future is Coming in Reverse)* and *Les prédateurs enjolivés (The Embellished Predators)*, Christin compiled two excellent collections of short stories, chronicles of a dilapidated near future where his political and ecological preoccupations are obvious. This is where Dr Christin shines through Mr Linus. All science fiction, no matter how wild, ultimately leads back to our present. Politics and fiction are inseparable. And wasn't that already the idea when he contributed to an anthology titled *C'est la lune finale*?* Says it all, doesn't it?

*Never translated into English, this anthology by thirteen French sci-fi authors revolved around the theme of utopias and better tomorrows. The title is a pun on the French word for moon, *'lune'*, and a line from the socialist anthem *L'Internationale* – 'C'est la *lutte* finale'.

Valerian's very name originates in a novel by Nathalie Henneberg*. No need to go on, though. First because sci-fi was always built on this kind of borrowing, with each writer standing on his predecessors' shoulders. But mostly because Christin was able to transfigure those influences.

...REINVENTED THROUGH POLITICS...

'In sci-fi,' Christin explains, 'there are two major schools. The first is pessimistic. It's based on the threat of nuclear war, on the fear of cataclysms, or on the globalisation of evil and misery. On the contrary, the second school believes in rationalism and a bright future. It postulates that man will always be there. *Valerian* stands halfway between these two schools.' Indeed, the main characteristic of *Valerian* surely lies in this ambivalence.

Because, despite appearances, Valerian and Laureline's exploits mark the end of adventurers. Aren't the real heroes more often power or production struggles or, as Christin puts it, 'social forces at work'? Even though the adventure is still a pleasure to read, the real focus is more on the reflection than on the action. The investigation inexorably becomes a quest. In the words of writer and editor Gérard Klein, 'Galaxity's central, all-powerful position, imposing its order on space and time, is both an illusion and a mistake.'

THE CHAMPION OF CLASSIC SCI-FI...

Sci-fi was still an almost new idea in *bande dessinée*, and Christin chose to introduce it by building on the genre's existing motifs. He wasn't inventing anything when he reused the time machine of Herbert George Wells (and so many others after him!). His settings and backgrounds of galactic empires are steeped in space opera – steeped in the works of Jack Williamson, Edmond Hamilton or, closer to us, Jack Vance. And the time-travelling character is a classic too, its archetype being Poul Anderson's *Time Patrol* of course, although Christin is actually much closer to the *Foundation* series by Isaac Asimov. There are clear echoes of planet Trantor in Galaxity and Point Central.

Here and there, other similar observations crop up. Sunken New York recalls John Wyndham's *The Kraken Wakes*. The hollow world of *The Land Without Stars* echoes Edgar Rice Burroughs. And let's not forget that

*La Plaie [The Plague], Le Rayon Fantastique series No. 122. Hachette/ Gallimard, 1964. Nathalie Henneberg is considered to be one of the pioneers of heroic fantasy in France.

...AND ECHOING OUR PRESENT.

Under Christin's pen, every star-bound humanity has its own struggles and oppressed masses. Everywhere through space, the great conflicts are still there: nature/technology, hierarchy/anarchy, oppression/revolution. In that regard, the three titles present in this collected volume are exemplary. Each time, Valerian and Laureline are called upon to become righters of wrongs. And both step up in their own imperfect way – a very by-the-book Valerian contrasting with the more intuitive and sensitive Laureline – which occasionally ends up creating strife in the happy couple, adding to the story's main conflict.

Christin, a skilled dialectician and 'fan of Borges as well as Perec' thus creates for himself an opportunity to express the whole spectrum of possible answers. And, more importantly, to deliver his message: 'Because, for me, there is no story without a moral,' he confirms. Adventures in the future or on distant worlds, yes, but a moral for today – a good summary of Christin's whole intent. Therefore Valerian's time, paradoxical time traveller that he may be, is less the past and the future than the present: today's Earth is always at the centre of the dizzying spatio-temporal landscape. Christin's sci-fi is much more eloquent when discussing the present than when speaking of hypothetical futures. No matter the star or the sun, all light always projects the same shadow: those extraterrestrial cultures are each a lesson for our civilisation. Everywhere strife reigns; everywhere the eternal debate between freedom and alienation rages. Valerian's true character lies in these uncertainties.

THE OTHER CHRISTIN

Say 'Christin' to a *bande dessinée* buff and he'll answer 'Mézières' and 'Bilal'. But let's not miss the wood for the trees!

Yes, Christin gave birth to this series, *Valerian*, and some of Bilal's greatest hits such as *The Black Order Brigade* and *Hunting Party*.

But how can we forget that he's also written for Tardi, Boucq, Vern, Max Cabanes, Patrick Lesueur, Jacques Ferrandez, Philippe Aymond, Jean-Claude Denis, Annie Goetzinger and André Juillard? This is not a complete list either, as it would stretch over sixty volumes touching on every genre, every leaning.

And yet the same obsessions are present in all of them. An avowed faith in expressing certain humanist values, a loathing of war and totalitarian systems, the rejection of aggression, a love of freedom and individuals, compassion for the meek and distrust in the mighty... All are permanent features of his work, along with one more essential aspect: a love of travelling.

Christin is a nomad at heart: 'To see and to remember' could be his motto. Which explains why the man has already been around the globe twice, and why you could meet him in Patagonia as easily as in Romania, Burma or the North Cape. Everywhere, though, he carries notebooks with him to jot down his dreams. 'This is where I find the best part of my inspiration,' he says.

Yet it's in his little corner of rural France that he takes the time to go on long walks (with, in the right season, porcini mushrooms as the goal) or write longer pieces (last novel to date: *Petits Crimes Contre les Humanités*). And it's in Paris that he lives life to the full, with friends, films, music, cycling...

Humanism, country- and culinary-style.

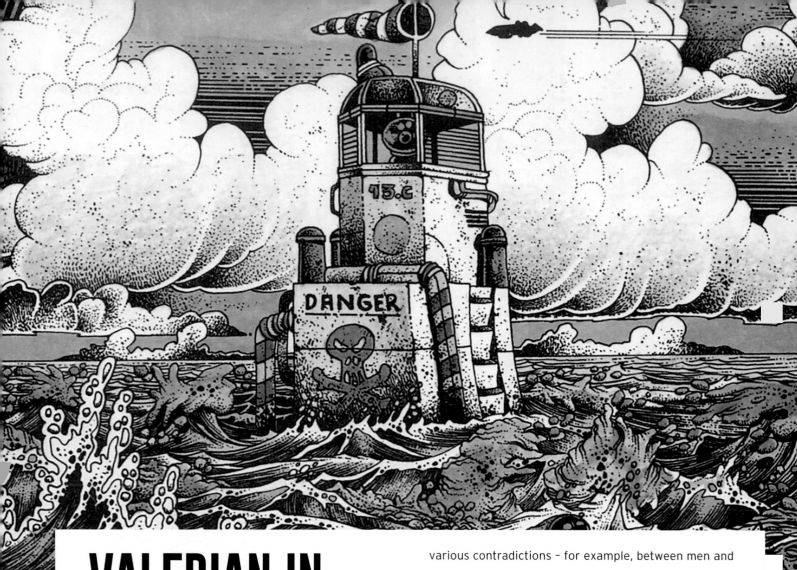

VALERIAN IN HIS OWN TIME

IN THE '70s – THE DECADE THAT SAW THE ADVENTURES OF VALERIAN AND LAURELINE COME INTO THEIR OWN – CHRISTIN BEGAN TO EXPLORE, IN VARIOUS WAYS AND THROUGH ALL MANNER OF GRAPHICAL OR NARRATIVE GENRES, THE BRUTAL TRANSFORMATIONS IMPACTING THE ERA...

In *Séjour en France (A trip to France)*, a civilisation textbook for American students illustrated by Jean-Claude Mézières, Christin describes a country that is no longer that of the baguette and the beret, still too often the prevailing image in the US, but rather a place of various contradictions – for example, between men and women, as in *The Land Without Stars*.

In bande dessinée, he wrote *Rumeurs sur le Rouergue* (*Rumours in Rouergue country*, initially published in *Pilote* in 1971), with Jacques Tardi on art duties; a story about the coming of multinationals and the foretold end of the traditional world – themes visibly similar to those in *Welcome to Alflolol*.

In literature, there were a string of short stories published in sci-fi magazines *Fiction* and *Galaxie*, and later collected under the title *Le futur est en marche arrière* (*The Future is Coming in Reverse*), with a cover by Mézières. Those were deliberately alarmist texts that denounced psychogenetic modifications and media manipulations - topics that were rarely touched upon at the time outside science-fiction works or scientific journals but that are present under slightly different guises in *Birds of the Master*.

Another warning call in another little-known field, environmentalism, was *En attendant le printemps* (*Waiting for Spring*), co-written by Patrick Lesueur, a collection of punchy short stories published in *Pilote* that depicted, among other things, manufacturing plants just as foul as those in *Welcome to Alflolol*.

And soon came the beginning of Christin's marvellous partnership with Enki Bilal for a series of graphic novels known under the generic title *Légendes d'aujourd'hui* (*Legends of Today*) – a promise in and of itself. In a part fantastic, part realistic, part political, part sociological fashion, they denounced the ravages of a technocratic modernity on an old nation that was rather set in its ways, such as France. Their contemporary, decidedly darkly humorous version of our future world contrasts with the gently rose-tinted irony of *Valerian*.

The denunciation of birds of ill omen – those of the 'Master', of course – is never far removed from equally impassioned claims to the right to happiness. That right found its perfect expression in an anthology of stories published, as always, in *Pilote* and illustrated by Jean Vern (Christin's brother in music and utopia), and given the prophetic title *En douce le bonheur* (*Happiness on the Sly*).

AND MEANWHILE...

THAT WAS JUST GREAT...

WHAT WAS GREAT!?!

THAT LITTLE MECHANICAL FAILURE, FOLLOWED BY CRASHING THE SHIP IN SO MUCH MUD THE BAY DOORS ARE BLOCKED—AND THE SKIFFS WITH THEM...

A FAILURE... I'M NOT SO SURE.

THERE WAS SOMETHING ELSE... I SAW SOMETHING GO BY, LIKE ... ER ... LIKE A DARK CLOUD. I PASSED OUT FOR AN INSTANT, AND...

AND NOW WE'RE IN THIS CRAP!

PAH! WATCH IT!

IF YOU THINK IT'S EASY!... EVERYTHING'S SLIMY, AND THIS SORRY EXCUSE FOR A RAFT ISN'T EXACTLY ...

THE CURRENTS ARE STRONG, TOO...

...Mézières, always a demanding taskmaster to himself and notorious for his difficulties in starting a new volume, will redraw these two opening pages of *Birds of the Master* entirely.

VALERIAN

FOREWORD TO THE 1981 US EDITION OF *AMBASSADOR OF THE SHADOWS*, BY WILL EISNER

Since *Famous Funnies* first appeared on US newsstands in the middle '30s the comic book as a publication has served as a vehicle for an unique form of graphic literature which we have been calling 'sequential art'. Today these 'comics' have reached a level of technology and audience encompassment that is allowing its writers and artists to contribute to an output no longer imprisoned in the narrow world of 'junk reading'.

Working in an international arena the practitioners of this art form are, as never before, enjoying (or struggling) with a greater professional status in the cultural community. They are producing work of increasing sophistication and they are pushing the boundaries of its potential with almost nuclear force.

As in the case of all artistic development, the core of such explosions shift. But for the moment the scene of greatest ferment is in France.

Recently, in a conversation with a colleague (Harvey Kurtzman) we explored the phenomenon of the 'comic' scene in France. We could agree that France, for the last ten years, has been the spearhead of the thrust. But the reasons for this were not so easily discerned and, I might add, are not easy (for Americans) to evaluate. You see, for almost 80 years, the United States was the fountainhead of the flow of comics that spread over the globe. From *Mutt & Jeff* to *Mickey Mouse* and *Buck Rogers*, and from *Terry and the Pirates* to *Superman*, it seemed that the prime source of direction came from North America. To get an overview, therefore, one has to regard the scene from atop this mighty monument. Not so easy to do.

Climate is one overriding factor in change and growth. In France, beginning with the seventies, two conditions served as incubators for a kind of genetic change in the direction of comic books. One was France's long history of intellectual ferment and the other was its liberal accreditation of comic book artists.

So as the radiation from the 'underground comic' explosion in the States spread to Europe, it germinated a whole body of new talent in the receptive gel of French culture.

Starting with the evolution of the magazine *Pilote* and the immense success of *Asterix* throughout the world, and continuing with the 'break-out' of artists such as Moebius and Druillet for *Heavy Metal*, and of Gotlib and others into independent ventures, a whole new thrust developed which impacted on the world scene. Just as the Spanish comic book artists had an enormous influence on the craft, the French pushed the intellectual level to new heights. It is from here, I firmly believe, that the new direction is proceeding. This is the orientation of future comic book art. We can see its influence in the American scene today.

It is always difficult (if not downright foolhardy) for a practitioner to attempt to name the 'best' or the 'most important' of his contemporaries. It is a lot more realistic (and safer) to admire ability. I therefore point with admiration to one of the French comic book teams in the vanguard of this exciting scene – a team which is clearly in possession of the qualities that are influencing this movement.

The work of Jean-Claude Mézières and Pierre Christin embodies a wonderful balance of intellect and craft that combines a kind of 'completeness'. They produce a comic page that is structurally whole. Mézières' architecture has the 'feel' of Windsor McCay with its towering knowledge of perspective and the solidity of construction. His futuristic scenes in *Valerian* for example have a believability equal to the realism of his people that live there. He imbues his people with a kind of grace and orchestrates their activity with great intelligence. As a comic book team, Christin and Mézières work with what I regard as the best combination of qualities... intelligence and discipline and imagination.

I commend their efforts to you.

Famous American cartoonist, Will Eisner (1917 - 2005) was a leading figure in the industry. The Comic Hall of Fame, and the prestigious Eisner Awards, are named in his honour.

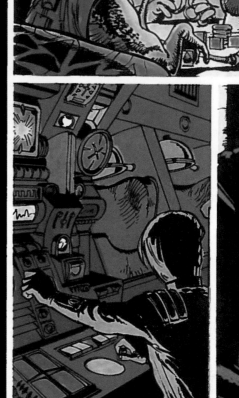

I.S.B.N. 2.205 06949-7

Back cover of the 1981 US edition of *Ambassador of the Shadows*

VALERIAN
A SCIENCE-FICTION COMIC-STRIP 'À LA FRANÇAISE'
INTRODUCTION TO THE 1981 US EDITION OF *AMBASSADOR OF THE SHADOWS*, BY DANIEL RICHE

Think back to 1975 when *Star Wars* and *Alien* had yet to be made. In England, a certain Chris Foss was beginning to make quite a name for himself, and the marvellous spacecraft from *2001 A Space Odyssey* filled us with wonder. A new S.F. esthetic was slowly emerging. At the time, the good old rockets of yesteryear and scenery drawn with the requisite curvy lines inherited from the '50s still predominated in most comics. And yet, even then things were starting to evolve…

First published in France, *Ambassador of the Shadows* was the sixth album in the adventure series, *Valerian Spatio-Temporal Agent*, created by Jean-Claude Mézières and Pierre Christin. The series had already been running for almost eight years. Its success in Europe showed that it was regarded by fans as one of the best S.F. series. Even then, Mézières and Christin were starting to get a following.

Valerian's originality lies not only in the profound humanism that permeates Christin's text and the 'anti-heroic' quality of the main character, although these elements are not negligible. Nor does it rely on *Laureline*, Valerian's companion, who is without a doubt one of the most non-conformist female characters in the history of comic books. To my mind, what is basically a question of originality – and originality there certainly is – owes a lot to Mézières' creations: machines, scenery and creatures. Obviously when we read *Ambassador of the Shadows* today in 1981, we no longer have that sense of disorientation we felt when we first discovered it. The decks of Point Central are haunted by machines, vessels and even stranger beings which now seem quite familiar to us. But remember 1975…

THE EMPIRE OF A THOUSAND PLANETS - 1970

A FEW DAYS LATER, AS THE GUILD'S CONVOY IS HEADING BACK TO SYRTE, CARRYING SLOHM'S FORMER PRISONERS…

IN THE FLOODED STREETS OF NEW YORK, THE LAUNCH SLOWLY THREADS ITS WAY THROUGH THE UNHEALTHFUL VEGETATION THAT FLOURISHES IN THE SWELTERING HEAT...

THE CITY OF SHIFTING WATERS · 1969

Then we didn't run the risk of confusing Valerian's craft with Han Solo's *Millennium Falcon* since Solo hadn't been invented yet. And as far as Point Central and its strange inhabitants are concerned, weren't they the forerunners of Mos Eisley's cantina and its bizarre patrons? Beyond a doubt, it's this avant-garde element that constitutes one of the series' primary qualities. Sooner or later people will realise that the S.F. esthetic which dominates the silver screen, book jackets and comic book art now at the beginning of the '80s, owes as much to Mézières' and Christin's comic books as it does to Kubrick's film. The proof of this is that you'll find certain frames of *Valerian* reproduced line for line in some French and foreign comic books. The price of glory... The fact remains that the creation of a universe is no easy task, and yet that is precisely what Mézières and Christin have been doing now for thirteen years. If the very face of science-fiction has evolved over the last few years, then we should not forget that it is partly thanks to them.

Daniel RICHE

WELCOME TO ALFLOLOL · 1972

Daniel Riche (1949 - 2005) was a French journalist, author and television screenwriter. He was also contributor and editor of several science-fiction magazines and collections for multiple publishers, and wrote a number of essays on comics and science-fiction.

THE STORIES IN THIS BOOK

'WITH THESE THREE VOLUMES THE READER JUMPS STRAIGHT INTO SPACE EXPLORATION, CHARACTERISTIC OF THIS FIRST PART OF THE SAGA. TO EACH VOLUME A PLANET, ITS FAUNA, ITS PEOPLE…' PIERRE CHRISTIN

THE LAND WITHOUT STARS –1972

At the edge of the universe, a rogue planet threatens Terran colonies. Called upon to help, Valerian and Laureline discover a strange world where the war of the sexes rages … literally. The two explorers split up to tackle the problem, each in their own way – one ever the action man, the other a high priestess of charm. Will they be able to prevent the impending disaster? In this volume, one of the most poetic in the series, Christin and Mézières are prolific creators. The former invents a hollow planet torn apart by war – an ideal canvas for a tale lambasting chauvinism and extreme feminism in equal measure! Simultaneously, Mézières perfectly illustrates that gorgeous, fantastic world where flowers are weapons… And his brush proves equally adept at painting this universe filled with house-carrying centipedes, vast, squalid cities, sumptuous palaces and giant insect battles as it does at revealing Laureline's charms: the girl from 1000 AD delivers one of her first seduction offensives – 'I like missions where we get to wear costumes,' she admits candidly.

WELCOME TO ALFLOLOL –1972

Technorog is an uninhabited planet blessed with limitless resources, which Galaxity has taken to exploit intensively – one might say plunder. Everything is perfect in the best of productionist worlds until a strange people, back after a 4,000-year-long trip, return to claim their planet – Technorog's name is actually Alflolol! It doesn't take long for the situation to become a hopeless mess…
Mézières and Christin raise the banner of political ecology. How to reconcile progress, an unforgiving productionist society and the rights of a people who live in harmony with nature? This tale (which cannot help but bring Native Americans to mind) could have been dreary. Instead it is joyous, thanks to the colourful gumun

> I'M GOING TO GO PITCH MY DOME SOMEWHERE AROUND HERE AND WAIT... WHAT ELSE CAN I DO? THE TRUTH IS, I'M NO LONGER NEEDED...

BIRDS OF THE MASTER – 1973

On an inhospitable planet, masses of slaves, watched by the menacing Birds of Madness, toil endlessly to feed the 'Master'. Marooned, then rescued at the last second, Valerian and Laureline find themselves among those hordes resigned to their captivity. Yet, spurred on by their presence, a resistance emerges...

The dialectics of domination and revolt! With this volume, resolutely placed under the banner of the struggle against oppression, Christin writes one of his most openly political scripts. In passing he offers some of the keys to his analysis of power struggles: dictatorship relies on the domination of minds (see especially page 167!) and only the pulling together of wills can bring an end to dictatorship. Using superb, shadow-filled purple and violet colours, Mézières illustrates it brilliantly, establishing a heavy, gloomy mood to better paint that world of woe. We're far from a left-wing propaganda treatise, though. Christin has far too much of a sense of humour for that! Proof of it rests in the two philosophers, the Stoic and the Marxist who, like a Greek chorus, constantly punctuate the action with their nonsense. And perhaps an even better proof is that ending, like a final thumbing of the nose – don't miss the final panel!

and iconoclastic boisterousness of the hard-partying troublemakers whose names are Argol, Garol, Orgal, Logar and Lagor! And yet the situation is most serious. The battle between hardliners and pure-of-hearts drives a wedge between our heroes. The wiser Laureline rebels and gives a meek Valerian the brush-off, siding firmly with the 'space bums'. 'The truth is, I'm no longer needed', laments Valerian... For the first time, this story introduces a real dynamic between Laureline, the brains, and Valerian, the brawn. But above all it asks a few essential questions from the halfway point between fable and adventure. How much can industry put a planet at risk? Is work truly a necessity?

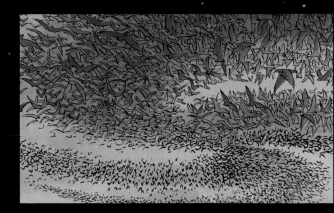

THE LAND WITHOUT STARS

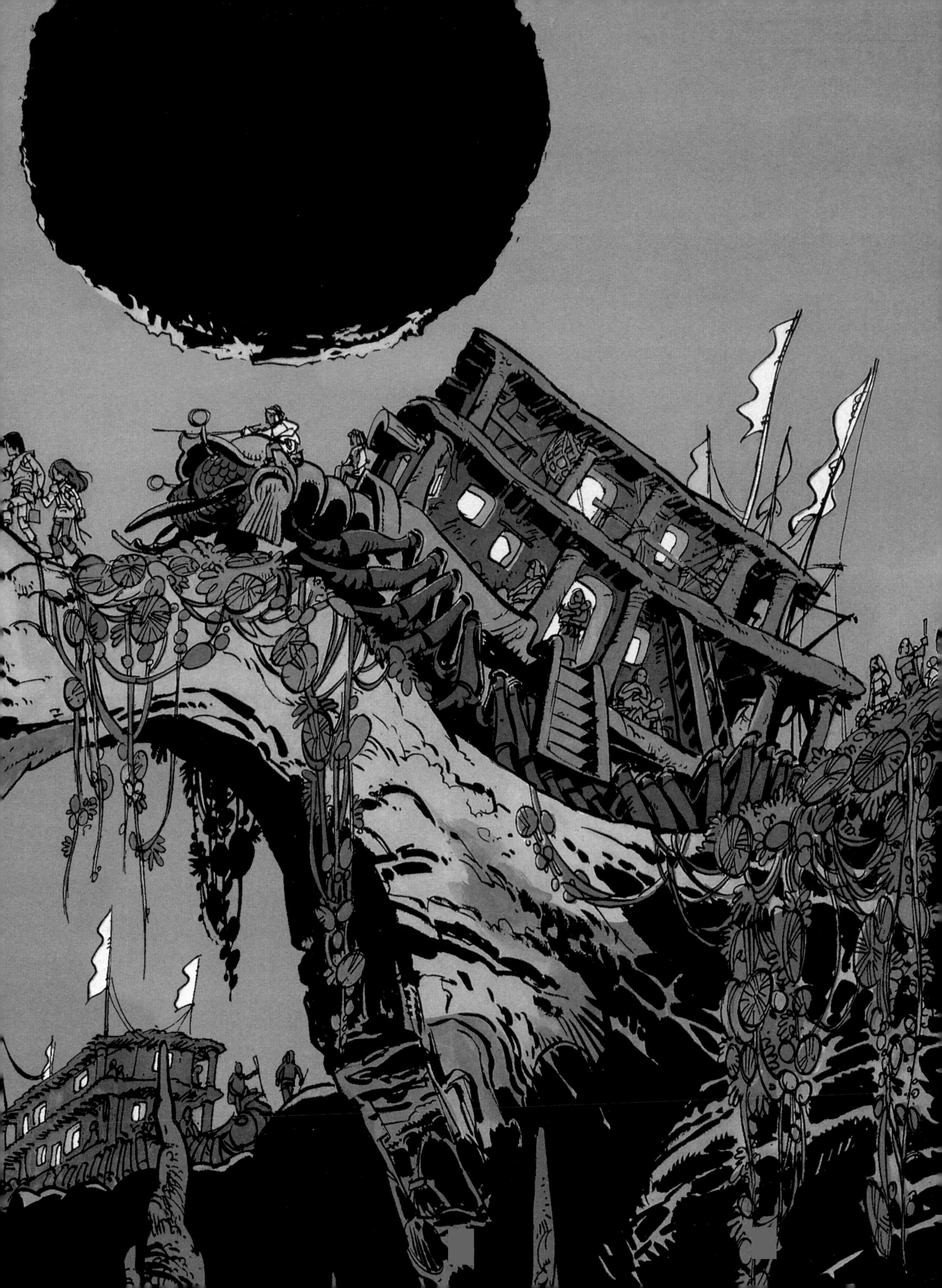

SOMEWHERE AT THE EDGE OF THE GALAXY... THE SMALL SOLAR SYSTEM OF **UKBAR** MARKS THE LIMIT OF THE EXPLORED UNIVERSE. BEYOND IT IS THE BLACK, OPPRESSIVE EMPTINESS OF SPACE.

ON THE FOUR PLANETS THAT ORBIT THEIR WARM STAR, A FEW HUNDRED TERRAN COLONISTS HAVE JUST BUILT THEIR NEW HOMES. PIONEERS, LOST THOUSANDS OF LIGHT-YEARS AWAY FROM THE HOME WORLD...

... THE LAST PRESENCE STILL CONNECTING THEM TO DISTANT EARTH IS ALMOST GONE. THE OFFICIAL SPACESHIP OF THE SPATIO-TEMPORAL SERVICE, AFTER ACCOMPANYING THEM ON THEIR JOURNEY AND HELPING THEM SETTLE, HAS BEGUN ITS FAREWELL TOUR...

ABOARD IT, TWO YOUNG AGENTS SENT BY **GALAXITY**, CAPITAL OF THE TERRAN EMPIRE: **VALERIAN AND LAURELINE.**

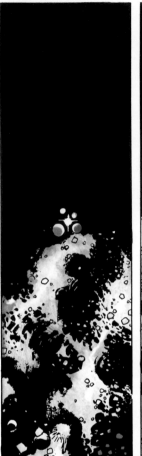

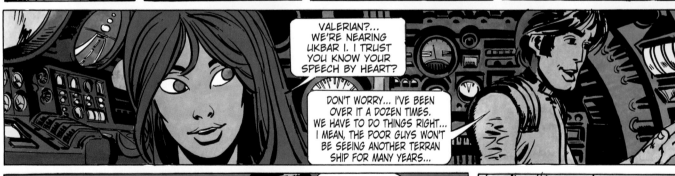

VALERIAN?... WE'RE NEARING UKBAR I. I TRUST YOU KNOW YOUR SPEECH BY HEART?

DON'T WORRY... I'VE BEEN OVER IT A DOZEN TIMES. WE HAVE TO DO THINGS RIGHT... I MEAN, THE POOR GUYS WON'T BE SEEING ANOTHER TERRAN SHIP FOR MANY YEARS...

OH, THEY DON'T SEEM TOO WORRIED BY THAT! THEY'RE WELL EQUIPPED AND SHOULD DO QUITE FINE HERE.

LET'S HOPE SO... GO GET READY WHILE I PREPARE THE APPROACH TO THE SPACEPORT...

We're glad to welcome you here one last time. Your help was invaluable...

Everyone's waiting for your speech...

Well, let's go, then. I'm just going to improvise, you know...

2A

... And to all of you, in the name of Earth, in homage to your endeavour, and seeing in your courage the very model of the values that alone must shape the philosophy of Terran expansion, I wish you good luck!

Hmm... A bit pompous, but not bad.

Yes, I'm fairly happy with it...

This way—the banquet is ready!

Suddenly, amidst the lively chatter of the merry revellers...

Psst! Come with me! I need to show you something...

2B

IS SOMETHING WRONG?

OH, NOT AT ALL... QUITE THE OPPOSITE.

I JUST WANTED TO GIVE YOU A TASTE OF THE FIRST ALCOHOL DISTILLED ON UKBAR I. MADE FROM ALGAE!

HMM... A BIT WEIRD, ISN'T IT?

TRY IT! TELL ME WHAT YOU THINK OF IT AFTERWARDS...

A BIT LATER, IN SPACE...

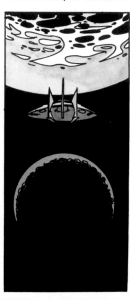

TUMTUM... TEETUM... CHARMING LITTLE AFFAIR! I HOPE THEY'LL BE AS WELCOMING ON UKBAR II. WE'RE ALMOST THERE.

YOU SOUND QUITE HAPPY FOR A FAREWELL MISSION...

GULP

QUITE TASTY, ACTUALLY!!

ANOTHER TASTE BEFORE YOU GO, THEN?

ON UKBAR II, AT THE END OF THE SECOND SPEECH...

... THE VERY MODEL OF THE VALUES THAT ALONE MUST SHAPE THE PHOLI... ER... THE PHILOSOPHY OF TERRAN EXPANSION, I WISH YOU GOOD LUCK!

SHALL WE LEAVE THE WOMEN TO IT? YOU CAN COME TRY THE RESULT OF OUR FIRST EXPERIMENTS!

WHAT KIND OF EXPERIMENTS?...

PHEW... LOVELY! QUITE REMARKABLE!

EN ROUTE TO UKBAR III...

VALERIAN! WHAT ARE YOU DOING?! CAN'T YOU SEE WE'RE GOING TO MISS THE PLANET BY 100,000 MILES?

OH? BAH, NO WORRIES, LITTLE LADY! A QUICK COURSE CORRECTION, AND... ALL GOOD!

31

AND ON THAT PLANET...

... THE VERY MODEL OF THE LAVUES... ER... VALUES THAT ALONE CAN SHAPE THE SILO... THE LIPHO... THE... ER... ANYWAY, YOU GO, BOYS, WE'LL BE CHEERING FOR YOU ALL THE WAY! YEEHAAA!!!

SO?...

GREAT, PAL! ONE MORE FOR THE ROAD AND THEN I'VE GOTTA GO...

DEPARTURE TIME...

BY SPACE! NOW I UNDERSTAND WHERE YOU KEPT DISAPPEARING TO! YOU'RE DRUNK AS A SKUNK!!

WHADDYA MEAN, DRUNK? I TRIPPED... COULD'VE HAPPENED TO ANYONE!

FINALLY, ABOVE UKBAR IV...

4A

VALERIAN, LET ME FLY THE SHIP! YOU'RE GOING TO MAKE US LOOK LIKE FOOLS!!!

QUIET, WOMAN!!! FOR OUR LAST PLANET, I'M GONNA GIVE THEM THE KIND OF ACROBATIC LANDING THAT'LL MAKE IT INTO THE HISTORY BOOKS!!!

VALERIAN! WE'RE GOING TO HIT!!!

... HIT WHAT?...

CRINNNGG

HEH HEH HEH!!! THAT WAS A FUN LANDING!

LOOK AROUND YOU, YOU BOOZE HOUND... THERE'S NO ONE HERE!! SOMETHING WEIRD IS GOING ON...

4B

THE BUFFET... ABANDONED!!

YOOHOO!...

SOMEONE... OVER THERE, AT THE OBSERVATORY...

WELL, LET'S GO... I WANNA GIVE MY SPEECH!

WHAT HAPPENED?!

COME SEE FOR YOURSELF!...

THERE'S A ROGUE PLANET HURTLING STRAIGHT TOWARDS US FROM DEEP SPACE! OUR ASTRONOMERS JUST LOCATED IT...

THIS MEANS **THE IMMINENT DESTRUCTION OF UKBAR!!!** TAKE A LOOK...

WHEN IT BARGES INTO OUR SYSTEM, WE CAN EXPECT THE MOTHER OF ALL COSMIC PINBALL GAMES...

WHAT TO DO?...

A SPEECH...

OH, YOU!! DON'T YOU UNDERSTAND THAT ALL THESE POOR PEOPLE CAME HERE ONLY TO DIE IN A MASSIVE CATACLYSM?! AND NOW THAT THE CARGO SHIPS HAVE BEEN DISMANTLED, WE CAN'T EVEN EVACUATE THEM!!!

OH, IS THAT ALL?...

WELL... HIC!... EARTH WILL NOT FAIL IN ITS DUTY, GOOD PEOPLE... ER... THE SPATIO-TEMPORAL SERVICE WILL PROTECT YOU! THAT PLANET OUT THERE... ER... WE'RE GONNA MAKE SHORT WORK OF IT...

... LET'S GO!!!

BUT....?!? OH, WHAT THE HECK... WHAT ELSE COULD WE DO, ANYWAY?...

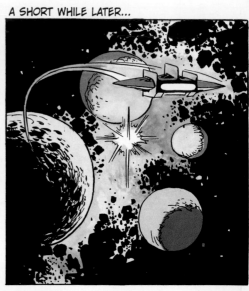

FINALLY, OFF UKBAR IV AND AFTER LONG PREPARATORY CALCULATIONS, COMES THE JUMP THROUGH SPACE-TIME...

ZZZZZZ

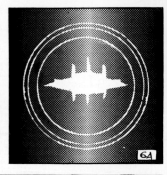

... THAT TAKES VALERIAN AND LAURELINE'S SPACESHIP ABOVE THE MYSTERIOUS PLANET STILL RACING ALONG ITS BLIND TRAJECTORY.

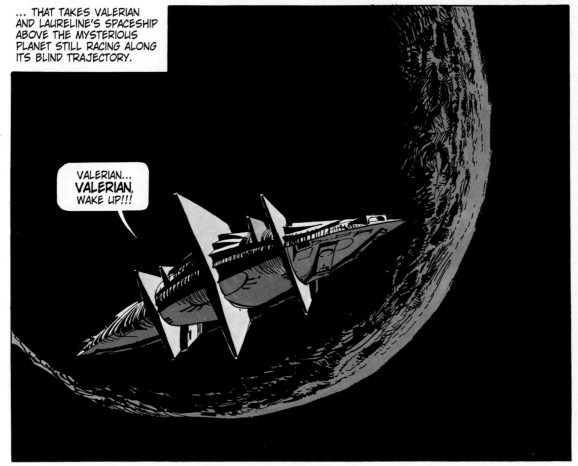

VALERIAN... **VALERIAN**, WAKE UP!!!

COME ON, GET UP!... WE'RE ABOUT TO LAND...

34

LAND WHERE?... OH, RIGHT... THAT PLANET THAT CAME OUT OF NOWHERE... OW!... MY BRAIN'S LIKE A FLUTMUL JELLYFISH!... DON'T WORRY, I'LL MANAGE...

A LITTLE LATER...

WHAT ARE WE DOING HERE?!... THIS PLACE IS LIKE A DRUNK'S NIGHTMARE...

EVERYTHING LOOKS DEAD...

WAIT... THERE'S LIGHT...

IT'S COMING FROM DOWN THERE...

SOMETHING IS RISING FROM THE BOTTOM!

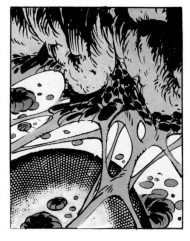

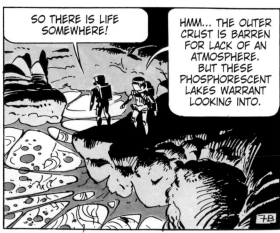

SO THERE IS LIFE SOMEWHERE!

HMM... THE OUTER CRUST IS BARREN FOR LACK OF AN ATMOSPHERE. BUT THESE PHOSPHORESCENT LAKES WARRANT LOOKING INTO.

WE'LL TAKE A SKIFF AND DIVE...

SOON, A STRANGE DESCENT BEGINS.

PLUNGING THROUGH INCREASINGLY ABUNDANT FLORA...

... THE SMALL CRAFT APPROACHES A LIGHT THAT GROWS BRIGHTER AND BRIGHTER...

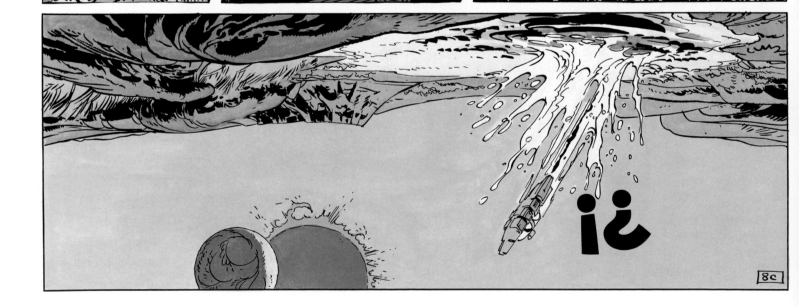

A HOLLOW PLANET!

THERE'S EVEN A MOON ORBITING IT!

ITS MOLTEN CORE ACTS AS ITS OWN SUN!

YES! LET'S TAKE ADVANTAGE OF ITS SHADE TO LAND IN THOSE HILLS OVER THERE...

WE'LL BE ABLE TO GET OUT. THERE'S A PERFECTLY BREATHABLE ATMOSPHERE.

BUT, AS THE SKIFF HOVERS SLOWLY TO FIND A LANDING SPOT...

THERE! SEE THAT?!

9A

HOUSES CARRIED BY ANIMALS!!!

THIS PLANET IS INHABITED!

APPARENTLY THEY'RE NOMADS.

HEY!... ONE OF THE... HOUSES IS FALLING... WE HAVE TO HELP THEM!

9B

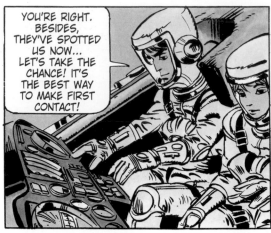

YOU'RE RIGHT. BESIDES, THEY'VE SPOTTED US NOW... LET'S TAKE THE CHANCE! IT'S THE BEST WAY TO MAKE FIRST CONTACT!

AND...

... MANOEUVRING DEFTLY, VALERIAN STRUGGLES TO STRAIGHTEN UP THE STRANGE CONSTRUCTION...

... WHILE THE NOMADS, PUSHING AND PULLING, GREET THIS UNEXPECTED HELP WITH MUCH SHOUTING.

FINALLY...

THAT'S IT! THEY'RE OUT OF THE WOODS...

I'M LANDING; WE'RE GETTING OUT... ARE THE SKIFF'S AUTOMATIC TRANSLATORS ON?

YES, AND THEY'VE ALREADY GATHERED ENOUGH LINGUISTIC MATERIAL TO ALLOW US TO COMMUNICATE...

SOON AFTERWARDS, BEFORE THE CROWD OF NOMADS, VALERIAN AND LAURELINE, ARMED ONLY WITH THEIR MINIATURISED TRANSLATORS, OPEN THE DIALOGUE...

WE ARE FRIENDS FROM ANOTHER WORLD...

ANOTHER WORLD? I DO NOT UNDERSTAND. BUT YOU ARE WELCOME AMONG THE LEMM PEOPLE. MY NAME IS MUTAHAR, AND I OFFER MY THANKS. YOU SAVED MANY LIVES TODAY...

WHAT HAPPENED?

OUR SKROMM—OUR ANIMAL-HOME, IF YOU WILL—STEPPED ON A FLOGUM HIDDEN IN THE GRASS... FORTUNATELY, THE EXPLOSION WAS VERY SMALL. THE FLOGUM HAD NOT MATURED YET.

DO YOU NOT KNOW WHAT A FLOGUM IS? THEN YOU REALLY AREN'T FROM THE WORLD OF ZAHIR... COME SEE!

LOOK. HERE IS A TINY ONE...

STRANGE. LOOKS LIKE A MINERAL POCKET...

AND HOW DID THESE... THINGS COME TO BE HERE?

THEY ARE FOUND ALL ALONG THE GREAT LUNAR CANYON.

I STILL DON'T GET IT...

IT IS SAID THAT THE RAYS OF THE MOON MAKE FLOGUMS GROW. SO, WE TRAVEL WITH OUR MOON. YEAR AFTER YEAR, WE COME BACK TO THE SAME PLACES. AND WHEN THE FLOGUMS ARE READY...

... WE TAKE THEM....

... LIKE THIS.

MUCH CARE IS REQUIRED. ONLY THE LEMM PEOPLE KNOW HOW TO EXTRACT FLOGUMS.

39

MAY I HAVE IT?

IF YOU WISH. IT IS WORTHLESS TO US. BUT, BE CAREFUL ANYWAY...

WHERE ARE ALL THESE FLOGUMS TAKEN?

TO OUR SKROMM-SHELTER. FOLLOW ME...

WHAT'S GOING ON OVER THERE?

WE'VE RESUMED THE EXTRACTION. IT'S A VERY RICH LODE THIS YEAR.

12A

WE KEEP THEM HERE, WELL PROTECTED.

AND THEN...?

WELL, WHAT ELSE? WHEN WE HAVE ENOUGH, WE SELL THEM TO THE POWERFUL CITIES OF VALSENNAR AND MALKA. THAT IS HOW THE LEMM PEOPLE EARN WHAT WE NEED TO FEED AND CLOTHE OURSELVES.

SUDDENLY, WHILE THE SMALL GROUP IS CHATTING AMIABLY...

... A POWERFUL SQUALL BLOWS THROUGH ZAHIR'S PEACEFUL ATMOSPHERE...

APART FROM THE FLOGUMS, THE GREAT CANYON IS BARREN...

WHAT?!

SSSSS

GET DOWN!

SSSSSHHHH

12B

ANOTHER ACCIDENTAL EXPLOSION?

NO! THIS IS JUST THE WAR...

THE WAR!?

OF COURSE! THE WAR BETWEEN VALSENNAR AND MALKA... WHAT DO YOU THINK THEY DO WITH THE FLOGUMS WE SEND THEM?...

I'M HEADING BACK TO THE SKIFF; WE CAN'T LEAVE IT UNATTENDED...

BAH! DO NOT WORRY. THIS WILL PASS!

ALL RIGHT! BUT BE CAREFUL!!

AND, AMIDST THE WHISTLING GUSTS THAT RIP THE AIR APART...

... AND OCCASIONALLY TEAR OFF WHAT GETS IN THE WAY OF THEIR STRANGE WHIRLWINDS...

YOU DON'T SEEM SURPRISED.

I AM USED TO IT. WAR HAS EXISTED FOR AS LONG AS ZAHIR HAS! BUT THE LEMM PEOPLE ARE PEACEFUL... AND WE ARE NEEDED BY BOTH SIDES... SO, WE ARE IN VERY LITTLE DANGER.

DO YOU HEAR? THE BATTLE WAS FAR AWAY, AND IT IS DRAWING STILL FARTHER AWAY. IT IS OVER.

YOU'RE NEEDED BECAUSE YOU'RE PROVIDING BOTH WARRING CITIES WITH DREADFUL WEAPONS!!!

OF COURSE... PARDON ME.

41

HO, MY FRIENDS! LET US PUT EVERYTHING BACK IN ORDER AND GET BACK TO WORK.

WE MUST COMPLETE OUR SHIPMENTS SO THAT OUR EXPEDITIONS TO VALSENNAR AND MALKA MAY LEAVE AS SOON AS POSSIBLE.

DON'T YOU REALISE THAT YOUR PLANET IS TUMBLING THROUGH SPACE!?! BY BEING ACCESSORIES TO THIS INTERMINABLE WAR, YOU...

PLANET?... SPACE?... I DO NOT UNDERSTAND WHAT YOU SPEAK OF. ANYWAY, THIS WAR IS NOT OF OUR DOING—WE DO NOT EVEN KNOW THE REASON FOR IT... WE SELL FLOGUMS—THAT IS ALL!

14A

WHAT NOW?

BUT, I...

AN EXPLOSION IN THE SKIFF!

YES! YOU SHOULD GO AND SEE WHAT IS HAPPENING OVER THERE...

LAURELINE!!! ARE YOU HURT?!

14B

NO, I'M FINE. BUT LOOK AT THE DAMAGE!

I TRIED TO EXAMINE THE LITTLE FLOGUM AND IT EXPLODED. OR RATHER...

... IT IMPLODED, **SUCKING IN** EVERYTHING AROUND IT. IN DOING SO, IT CAUSED EVERY ONE OF OUR ELECTROMAGNETIC INSTRUMENTS TO BLOW!

I DID HAVE A LOOK AT OUR SENSORS DURING THE BATTLE, THOUGH. ZAHIR'S MAGNETISM WAS COMPLETELY DISRUPTED. THE LEVEL OF ACTIVITY AT THE CENTRAL CORE WAS ABNORMAL. THE PLANET'S AXIS TILTED AND ITS FALL THROUGH SPACE ACCELERATED EVEN MORE...

HMMM... THIS PLANET MUST HAVE LEFT ITS ORIGINAL ORBIT AFTER ONE OF THE COUNTLESS BATTLES THE ZAHIRIANS HAVE BEEN FIGHTING SINCE THE DAWN OF TIME. THE BALANCE OF A HOLLOW WORLD LIKE THIS ONE MUST BE VERY PRECARIOUS.

WE HAVE TO DO SOMETHING!

YES... STOP THE WAR... ONLY THEN WILL WE BE ABLE TO TRY AND MAKE THE ZAHIRIANS, UNAWARE OF THE OUTSIDE WORLD AS THEY ARE, UNDERSTAND THAT THEY'RE HEADING FOR DISASTER.

WE CAN TAKE ADVANTAGE OF THE LEMM EXPEDITIONS TO GO SEE WHAT'S GOING ON. IT'LL BE EASY—OUR FRIEND MUTAHAR WON'T BE SORRY TO SEE US GO...

A BIT LATER...

YES, EVERYTHING IS ALMOST READY FOR DEPARTURE AND YOU MAY GO WITH THE EMISSARIES OF THE LEMM PEOPLE. BUT ON ONE CONDITION...

ONLY MEN MAY GO TO MALKA, AND ONLY WOMEN ARE ALLOWED INTO VALSENNAR. YOU MUST FOLLOW THE RULE.

BUT... WHY SUCH A RULE?

I DO NOT KNOW! IT HAS ALWAYS BEEN SO, AND THE LEMM PEOPLE ARE NOT CURIOUS. SO...

ALL RIGHT. WE WERE THINKING OF SPLITTING UP ANYWAY.

IN THE PARTIAL DARKNESS IN WHICH THE WRETCHED LEMM TRIBE IS CONDEMNED TO STAY FOREVER, ETERNALLY FOLLOWING THE SLOW MOVEMENT OF THE MOON'S SHADOW ALONG THE GREAT CANYON...

... THE LAST PREPARATIONS ARE BEING MADE.

NEAR THE HASTILY-REPAIRED SKIFF...

OK! RADIO, DISCREET OFFENSIVE AND DEFENSIVE WEAPONS FOR EACH OF US... I THINK THAT'LL DO.

16A

I LIKE MISSIONS WHERE WE GET TO WEAR COSTUMES.

YOU MAKE A VERY CONVINCING FLOGUM PEDLAR!! BY THE WAY, I'VE SPOTTED A KIND OF CAVERN ALONG THE CANYON WHERE WE CAN HIDE THE SKIFF.

SOON...

NOW WE CAN GO...

16B

44

AND...

SAFE TRAVELS!

SOON SEPARATED, VALERIAN AND LAURELINE...

... FIRST TRAVEL ALONG THE BARREN GREAT CANYON.

AFTER MANY HOURS OF RIDING, THEY COME OUT OF THE MOON'S SHADOW AT LAST AND INTO THE HARSH LIGHT OF ZAHIR'S SUN.

WITH ONE LAST GOODBYE, THE TWO EXPEDITIONS GO THEIR SEPARATE WAYS TOWARDS THEIR RESPECTIVE DESTINATIONS...

... LIVING OFF THE LAND, HUNTING AND FISHING FOR FRUGAL MEALS...

AND STOPPING ONLY FOR THE HOLLOW PLANET'S STRANGE RED NIGHT, DURING THE DAILY LULL IN THE OTHERWISE CONSTANT SOLAR ERUPTIONS.

WHEN WILL WE BE THERE?

SOON! THE CITY OF MALKA IS THE CLOSEST TO OUR CURRENT MINING FIELD...

45

INDEED, AFTER ANOTHER THREE DAYS' RIDE...

SO THIS IS MALKA!

YES. THERE ARE ONLY TWO CITIES IN ALL OF ZAHIR, BUT THEY ARE VERY BEAUTIFUL.

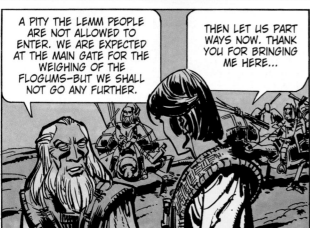

A PITY THE LEMM PEOPLE ARE NOT ALLOWED TO ENTER. WE ARE EXPECTED AT THE MAIN GATE FOR THE WEIGHING OF THE FLOGUMS—BUT WE SHALL NOT GO ANY FURTHER.

THEN LET US PART WAYS NOW. THANK YOU FOR BRINGING ME HERE...

MINGLING WITH THE CROWD THAT SURROUNDS THE LEMM EXPEDITION, VALERIAN TAKES A STROLL ALONG THE WALLS OF MALKA...

STRANGE... I SEE ONLY MEN HERE... AND FOR A CITY THAT LOOKS THIS RICH, THEY SEEM RATHER SCRUFFY...

WHAT'S FOR SURE IS THAT THE CITY'S WELL GUARDED! GETTING INSIDE ISN'T GOING TO BE EASY...

46

MUCH, MUCH LATER...

NOTHING. IT'S THE SAME EVERYWHERE!

UNLESS... THIS SEWAGE COMES FROM INSIDE. AT WORST, I'LL BE PUSHED BACK OUT BY THE CURRENT. I'LL RISK IT!

19A

STRUGGLING HARD AGAINST THE SWIRLING WATERS...

... VALERIAN IS RUNNING OUT OF AIR AND ABOUT TO BE SWEPT AWAY, WHEN...

... STRUCK BY ALL MANNER OF REFUSE THEY CARRY...

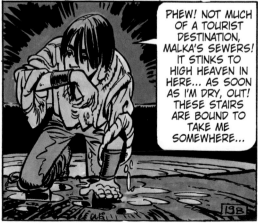

PHEW! NOT MUCH OF A TOURIST DESTINATION, MALKA'S SEWERS! IT STINKS TO HIGH HEAVEN IN HERE... AS SOON AS I'M DRY, OUT! THESE STAIRS ARE BOUND TO TAKE ME SOMEWHERE...

19B

INDEED...

STILL NOTHING BUT MEN. IT DOES MAKE THINGS EASIER FOR ME, BUT I'D LIKE TO UNDERSTAND...

... THEY SEEM TO BE DOING EVERYTHING AROUND HERE!

I WONDER WHAT EXACTLY IS WOMEN'S WORK IN THIS CITY!

?!

UH-OH... I THINK I'M ABOUT TO FIND OUT!

SINGLE LINE AGAINST THE WALL!!

AND QUICK!

HO, OVER THERE! TRYING TO RUN?!

MAYBE YOU DON'T KNOW THE PUNISHMENT?

A 'G

NO!

THAT WAS JUST A WARNING!

ENOUGH OF THIS! CHOOSE THE LEAST UGLY ONES! THEY'LL HAVE THE HONOUR OF FIGHTING AGAINST THOSE LIMP KLOFORS OF VALSENNAR IN OUR NEXT BATTLE!

BY SPACE! IF ONLY SOMEONE HAD TOLD ME THEY USED FORCED CONSCRIPTION IN MALKA!

YOU... AND YOU... AND YOU... AND YOU...

IT SERVES MY PURPOSE, ACTUALLY! ONCE IN THE ARMY, I'LL BE AT THE HEART OF THINGS. I ONLY HOPE THESE HARRIDANS FIND ME SUFFICIENTLY PLEASING...

HEY, THIS ONE'S LESS UGLY THAN THE OTHERS! TAKE HIM. THAT'LL BE ENOUGH FOR TODAY.

BEING REDUCED TO SUCKING UP. HOW HUMILIATING...

TWO COLUMNS! NO TALKING! TO THE BARRACKS OF THE THOUSAND FEMININE VIRTUES! FORWARD!!!

AND, WITH A GREAT CRACKING OF WHIPS, THE GROUP MAKES ITS WAY TOWARDS MALKA'S MILITARY DISTRICT...

FINALLY...

YOU ARE IN WHAT WILL BE YOUR PERMANENT BILLET. YOUR INSTRUCTION WILL BEGIN NOW...

THROUGHOUT AN EXHAUSTING DAY, VALERIAN AND HIS UNFORTUNATE FELLOWS DISCOVER MALKA'S HORRIBLE ARSENAL. FLAME-THROWING KUCHUKS...

... VENOM-SPITTING TALAMS...

... KLAMIPS AND THEIR KNIFE-LIKE TONGUES...

... DEADLY GRIFF CANNONS...

WITH NO REGARD FOR THE MANY ACCIDENTS...

... THE MERCILESS WARRIOR WOMEN PUNISH THE CLUMSY AND THE UNWILLING.

J.C. MÉZIÈRES 23

51

AT LAST, THAT NIGHT, OVER A REVOLTING STEW...

BAH... FROM THE MOMENT YOU'RE PICKED UP, YOU'RE AS GOOD AS DEAD ANYWAY. EVERY BATTLE KILLS NINE TENTHS OF THE MEN WHO FIGHT IN IT...

I'M BEAT!

BUT... ER... WHY ARE WE AT WAR WITH VALSENNAR?

HUH?!... WHERE'S HE FROM, THIS ONE? DID YOU BANG YOUR HEAD OR SOMETHING?

DON'T YOU KNOW THAT IN VALSENNAR IT'S THE MEN WHO ARE IN CHARGE? THEY SAY LIFE IS HORRIBLE IN THAT LOUSY CITY OF THEIRS...

YOU BET IT'S HORRIBLE! AND THAT'S WHY WE'RE GONNA FIGHT AGAIN! HERE, AT HOME, WOMEN PROTECT CIVILISATION...

... AND THAT'S HOW IT SHOULD BE. AIN'T THAT RIGHT, EVERYONE?

YEP... I'LL TELL YOU, THOUGH: THE SOONER WE CROAK, THE BETTER...

... 'CAUSE AFTER THE BATTLES, IF YOU SURVIVE, THEY SEND YOU TO THE PALACE OF THE SUPREME FEMININITY FOR A PROCREATION SESSION. I HEAR IT'S WORSE THAN ANYTHING...

STILL... HAVE YOU... I MEAN, HAVE WE, THE MEN OF MALKA, ALWAYS BEEN... ER... TREATED LIKE THIS?

YOU'VE REALLY CRACKED YOUR HEAD! MALES ARE INFERIOR- EVERYONE KNOWS THAT!

WE'RE JUST GOOD ENOUGH TO CARRY FLOGUMS THAT'LL BLOW UP IN OUR FACES, TAKE CARE OF THE KIDS AND CLEAN UP THE CITY. IT'S TRUE...

AREN'T YOU DONE YAPPING LIKE A BUNCH OF VALSENNAR SISSIES IN HERE!? LIGHTS OUT! TRAINING RESUMES TOMORROW, YOU WIMPS!

NOW, NOW, NO NEED TO GET WORKED UP...

YOU WATCH YOUR MOUTH, PRETTY FACE!

WELL, AREN'T I IN A PICKLE! TO THINK IT'S ALWAYS BEEN A WAR OF THE SEXES BETWEEN VALSENNAR AND MALKA! NO WAY I CAN CALL LAURELINE IN THESE CONDITIONS. I GUESS THE BEST THING TO DO FOR NOW IS... SLEEP.

MEANWHILE, THE CONVOY OF LEMM WOMEN THAT LAURELINE IS TRAVELLING WITH IS REACHING THE END OF ITS LONG JOURNEY...

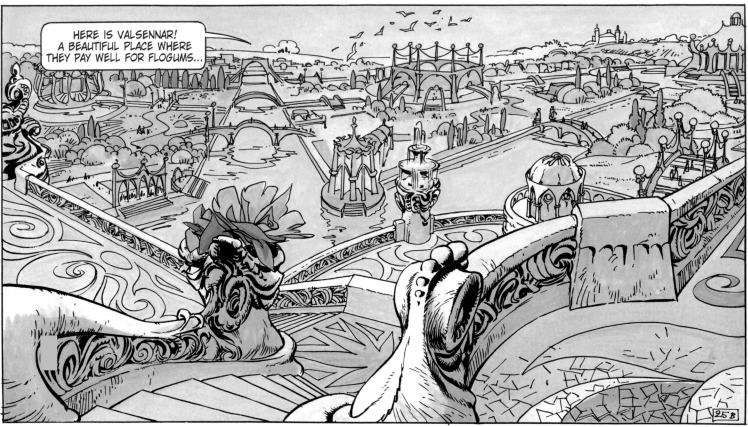

HERE IS VALSENNAR! A BEAUTIFUL PLACE WHERE THEY PAY WELL FOR FLOGUMS...

AND, ONCE PAST THE CITY DOORS...

TIME TO SAY GOODBYE...

YES, WE MUST GO A LITTLE FURTHER TO DELIVER OUR FLOGUMS...

THANK YOU FOR YOUR HELP. HAVE A SAFE TRIP BACK—I'M STAYING.

HMM... LOVELY PLACE, VALSENNAR. VALERIAN WOULD LOVE IT... WOMEN SEEM TO BE WORKING HARD HERE.

WANDERING THE SUNNY STREETS OF THE CITY, LAURELINE HAPPENS UPON SOME STRANGE SHOPS...

WHEN...

DID YOU COME FOR THE CONTEST TOO, MY CHILD?

ME? ER...

THEN YOUR LUCK HAS BROUGHT YOU TO THE RIGHT SHOP. FOLLOW OLD NADJIKA IF YOU WANT TO WIN. OUR LORDS AND MASTERS DON'T LIKE YOKELS WHO SMELL OF MANURE! COME...

OH? THAT'S INTERESTING... BESIDES, I'M NO UGLY DUCKLING, AFTER ALL...

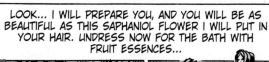

LOOK... I WILL PREPARE YOU, AND YOU WILL BE AS BEAUTIFUL AS THIS SAPHANIOL FLOWER I WILL PUT IN YOUR HAIR. UNDRESS NOW FOR THE BATH WITH FRUIT ESSENCES...

IF YOU WIN, YOU WILL GO TO THE PALACE. ONCE THERE, YOU WON'T FORGET OLD NADJIKA, WILL YOU?... I'VE ALWAYS BEEN TOO UGLY TO WIN...

I PROMISE, NADJIKA...

HURRY! THE TRIALS WILL BEGIN SOON!

THE TRIALS!? WHOA! I...

COME NOW, YOU CANNOT START BEING AFRAID NOW: EVERYONE IS WATCHING YOU! EMPEROR ALZAFRAR HIMSELF IS HERE. HURRY ALONG...

AND, BEFORE THE DISTRACTED OR APPRAISING EYES OF THE COURT...

... THE TRIALS BEGIN.

DURING THE ENTIRE WARM VALSENNAR DAY, THE CONTEST GOES ON WITHOUT INTERRUPTION. COOKING, WEAVING, MUSIC...

BURNED!!... NO WONDER. WITH ALL THEIR READY-MADE JUNK AT THE SPATIO-TEMPORAL SERVICE, I'VE LOST MY TOUCH!

OH, DEAR. THIS IS THE FINAL NAIL...

TSK TSK... ON THE CONTRARY, IT'S VERY ORIGINAL. BRING HER TO ME!

HAVE YOU NOTICED THAT YOUNG WOMAN? SHE'S ABSOLUTELY CHARMING...

INDEED, MY PRINCE... BUT ALLOW ME TO SAY SHE SINGS LIKE A CRACKED GLOMUS!

THE EMPEROR HONOURS YOU, YOUNG WOMAN. HE SUMMONS YOU!

?! ARE YOU SURE?!

WELL DONE, YOUNG BEAUTY! I HAVE DECIDED THAT YOU WIN THE CONTEST!

WELL, I'LL BE...!

HEY! THE REST OF YOU! STOP THE TRIALS. AND IF THERE'S ANY WHINING FROM LOSING FEMALES, GIVE EVERY WOMAN HERE A GOOD BEATING! AND MAKE SURE EVERYONE GETS THE SAME.

AS FOR YOU, YOU'RE COMING WITH ME. THERE ARE GOING TO BE GREAT CELEBRATIONS AT THE PALACE. THOSE HORRIBLE VIRAGOS OF MALKA HAVE CHALLENGED US... BUT WE HAVE A FEW DAYS. UNTIL THEN, YOU CAN BASK IN THE BEAUTY OF OUR POETRY JOUSTS.

IS THIS YOUR CASTLE, MY PRINCE?

WHY, YES, PEASANT GIRL. THE PALACE OF RESPLENDENT VIRILITY

WHAT A GORGEOUS PLACE!

TRUE, TRUE. DESIGNED ENTIRELY BY ME, AND DECORATED BY MY DEAREST FRIENDS.

IF ONLY THOSE FAT COWS OF MALKA, SO BLIND TO BEAUTY, DIDN'T DROP FLOGUMS ON IT EVERY CHANCE THEY GET...

THERE'S ALWAYS SOMETHING TO REPAIR... AH, WELL. WE'LL GIVE THEM A GOOD THRASHING AT THE NEXT BATTLE.

AND WHAT'S THIS?

PART OF OUR WAR FLEET! WHAT CHOICE HAVE WE BUT TO DEFEND THE ETERNAL VALUES OF THE MIND AGAINST THE OBSCURANTIST BRUTALITY FROM THE OTHER SIDE OF ZAHIR?

BUT... THE FLEET... THESE WEAPONS... THEY'RE OPERATED BY WOMEN!?

WHERE DID YOU COME FROM, LITTLE BIRD BRAIN? WAR IS VIOLENT... DIRTY... LETHAL, EVEN. GOOD ONLY FOR WOMEN.

WE LIKE THE COLOURFUL SPECTACLE OF A PRETTY BATTLE! BUT YOU CANNOT POSSIBLY IMAGINE THAT WE WOULD STOOP SO LOW AS TO USE THESE DISGUSTING MILITARY OBJECTS OURSELVES, I HOPE! ANYWAY...

... ENOUGH TALK! NOW YOU WILL GO WITH YOUR FELLOWS AND TRY TO LOOK BEAUTIFUL FOR OUR DELICIOUS SOIREE.

LATER...

LAURELINE IN THE HAREM! A NEW EPISODE IN THE GLORIOUS LIFE OF A FEMALE SPATIO-TEMPORAL AGENT!... VALERIAN, MY BOY...

IF ONLY I COULD CALL TO TELL YOU WHAT I THINK OF YOU AND YOUR FELLOW MEN...

OH, WELL... I MIGHT AS WELL WIN THE FAVOUR OF THAT PRETENTIOUS LITTLE EMPEROR!

AND, AS NIGHT COMES, CELEBRATIONS BEGIN IN VALSENNAR WITH MANY LIBATIONS OF FLOWER ALCOHOL, AND CONTINUE UNINTERRUPTED FOR THE FOLLOWING DAYS, TO THE SOUND OF RARE POEMS AND DELICATE MUSIC...

TRAINING IN MALKA CONTINUES, AND AN EXHAUSTED VALERIAN DISCOVERS THE IMPRESSIVE WAR FLEET OF THE FORTIFIED CITY.

FIRST TASKED WITH LOADING THE FLOGUMS ONTO THE FAST FLYERS RESERVED FOR WOMEN-OFFICERS...

... HE'S SOON SENT TO ONE OF THE MASSIVE AERIAL VESSELS PACKED WITH HUNDREDS OF MEN COMMITTED TO THE MOST OBSCURE ROLES OF THE LOOMING BATTLE.

FINALLY, ON THE MORNING OF THE CHOSEN DAY...

LOOK CLOSELY, DOPEY! IF YOU'VE NEVER SEEN OUR QUEEN, SHE'S ABOUT TO PASS US ON THE WAY TO HER SHIP.

IS SHE PRETTY?

GORGEOUS! LOOK... THERE SHE IS WITH HER STAFF OFFICERS.

SOON AFTER, RISING MAJESTICALLY INTO THE AIR, PULLED BY TEAMS OF BEETLES WITH HUMMING WINGS, ALL SHIPS GREAT AND SMALL LEAVE THE POWERFUL CITY OF WOMEN...

LONG LIVE KLOPKA THE EXQUISITE!

WHOOPS! A PLEASURE TO GET KILLED FOR HER, INDEED!

... LED BY THE ROYAL VESSEL.

AT THE SAME MOMENT IN VALSENNAR, THE IMPERIAL FLEET IS ALSO TAKING FLIGHT.

ABOARD THE FLAGSHIP, WHICH REMAINS PRUDENTLY WITH THE REARGUARD, THE COURT PREPARES TO ENJOY THE SHOW.

AMIDST THE EXCITED COURTIERS SITTING IN THE SHADE OF A DAIS, A FEW YOUNG WOMEN SERVE REFRESHMENTS...

AND, UNDER ZAHIR'S SCALDING SUN, SKIMMING THE ROCKY SURFACE OF THE BARREN MOON, THE ENEMY FLEETS DRAW INEXORABLY NEARER TO EACH OTHER...

AND SOON THEY CLASH WITH APPALLING VIOLENCE. THE CARNIVOROUS GRENADES OF VALSENNAR COUNTER MALKA'S FLAME-THROWING KUCHUKS...

... AND, WITH GRAPPLING HOOKS QUICKLY BRINGING THE TROOPS TO HAND-TO-HAND COMBAT, CHOKING SNIARKS ANSWER PILIPS CROSSBOWS...

EVERYWHERE IN THE SKIES OF THE HOLLOW PLANET, THE BATTLE RAGES. THE FLOGUM-ARMED FLYERS HAVE GONE INTO ACTION AS WELL...

... AND AROUND THE INCREASINGLY UNSTABLE SUN, CONVULSING WITH MASSIVE TURBULENCE, ZAHIR'S ATMOSPHERE IS TORN BY TERRIFYING ERUPTIONS...

MEANWHILE, ON THE DECK OF THE VESSEL WHERE VALERIAN IS ENGAGED IN A BLOODY MELEE...

A RIDERLESS FLYER! NOW'S THE TIME FOR ME TO MAKE AN IMPRESSION ON KLOPKA THE EXQUISITE!

GOOD! FULL FLOGUM PAYLOAD... THE PILOT DIDN'T HAVE TIME TO USE IT.

THIS CREATURE SEEMS QUITE DOCILE... LET'S GO! THE ZAHIRIANS ARE GOING TO SEE WHAT A REAL PROFESSIONAL PILOT CAN DO.

VALERIAN QUICKLY FLIES INTO ACTION. LEAVING BE THE HEAVY VESSELS OVERLOADED WITH POOR WRETCHES OF BOTH GENDERS FORCED TO KILL EACH OTHER FOR A WAR THAT ISN'T THEIRS...

... HE CHARGES VALSENNAR'S FLYERS.

PUNCHING THROUGH THE ENEMY LINES WITH EASE, HE RUSHES TOWARDS THE EMPEROR'S CITY...

... AND HITS THE DESERTED PALACE WITH AN INCREDIBLY DESTRUCTIVE SALVO OF FLOGUMS...

WHILE, MUCH HIGHER IN THE SKY...

OH?... ONE OF OUR MEN DID THAT! I WANT THAT FANTASTIC FIGHTER BROUGHT TO ME AFTER THIS WONDERFUL BATTLE!

AAH! MY BEAUTIFUL PALACE!! BOOOOOHOOOOO!

DO NOT CRY, MY PRINCE! YOUR TROOPS HAVE BROKEN THROUGH AS WELL. THEY MUST BE BOMBING MALKA AS WE SPEAK.

AND...

IF I HAVEN'T BEEN NOTICED WITH THAT, IT'S HOPELESS! ALL I NEED NOW IS ONE LAST FEAT, LIKE...

... GIVING VAL-SENNAR'S FLAGSHIP A GOOD SCARE!

BUT... BUT... SOMEONE IS ATTACKING US!!!

THAT'S NEVER HAPPENED BEFORE! WHAT SORT OF A NEW WAY TO MAKE WAR IS THIS!?!

HELP!

WHAT'S THIS?!

A CROSSBOW! LEAVE IT!... OH, WHERE CAN WE HIDE?!

SCHTonk !

BAH! BUNCH OF PANSIES!... JUST WATCH THIS!

OH, NO! IT'S VALERIAN!!

MY LITTLE LAURELINE!! WHAT A WOMAN SHE IS...

SHOOTING ME DOWN ALL BY HERSELF! MY POOR MOUNT IS DONE FOR... AND SO AM I!

MAYBE NOT... THAT SHIP DRIFTING DOWN THERE...

IT'S A SLAUGHTERHOUSE! AND THIS ABNORMAL HEAT! THE SUN'S ACTIVITY IS OFF THE CHARTS. TO THINK THAT WHILE THE ZAHIRIANS BUTCHER EACH OTHER WITH OUR HELP, THEIR PLANET IS STILL HURTLING THROUGH SPACE!

ANYWAY. I SHOULD HAVE MADE MYSELF SUFFICIENTLY HEROIC NOW. BACK TO MALKA. I SEE THAT EVERYONE'S GOING HOME; THE BATTLE MUST BE OVER...

THAT VERY EVENING IN MALKA, WHILE SHOUTS OF VICTORY RISE TO THE WINDOWS OF THE PALACE OF SUPREME FEMININITY...

AND IN VALSENNAR, IN ONE OF THE UNDAMAGED WINGS OF THE PALACE OF RESPLENDENT VIRILITY...

ALONE IN MY PRIVATE CHAMBERS. THAT'S WHAT I CALL A PROMOTION! I CAN CALL LAURELINE...

SO, NOW I AM THE EMPEROR'S FAVOURITE FOR SAVING HIS LIFE!! BUT TO THINK IT ALMOST COST ME VALERIAN... I FEEL SICK! QUICKLY... I NEED TO KNOW IF HE'S OK!

VALERIAN!!

LAURELINE!

IT'S WONDERFUL TO HEAR YOUR VOICE! I WAS SO SCARED...

I WAS SCARED TOO... FOR YOU. BUT, LISTEN, WE HAVE TO MAKE THIS QUICK. I HAVE A PRIVATE AUDIENCE WITH THE QUEEN IN A FEW MINUTES...

HA! THAT'S FUNNY! THE EMPEROR IS EXPECTING ME IN AN ISOLATED PAVILION IN THE PARK FOR A LIGHT DINNER...

IS HE?

... WELL, AT LEAST THIS WAY WE CAN ACT AT THE SAME TIME. HERE'S MY PLAN. THE ZAHIRIANS ARE ALL WAR-CRAZY, RESIGNED TO THEIR FATE, OR OBLIVIOUS. THERE'S NO POINT IN TRYING TO CONVINCE THEM OF THE DANGER THEY FACE...

WE MUST STRIKE AT THE HEAD. TONIGHT, WE KIDNAP THE EMPEROR AND THE QUEEN. WITH THE CHAOS AROUND HERE, I WON'T HAVE ANY TROUBLE STEALING SOME SHIP OR OTHER.

WELL, WELL... JUST FOR YOUR INFORMATION, I'VE ALREADY HIDDEN ONE IN THE GARDENS NEAR THE PAVILION!

38A

I HAVE TO SAY, YOU'VE LEARNED A LOT FROM ME... ALL RIGHT, WE'LL MEET AT THE SKIFF AS SOON AS POSSIBLE. I'LL EXPLAIN THE REST LATER. GOOD LUCK, GORGEOUS!

TO YOU TOO. LOVE YOU!

A FEW MINUTES LATER, IN VALSENNAR...

AND HERE COMES OUR BRAVE WARRIORESS! COME, LAURELINE... AND YOU, LEAVE US.

AND IN MALKA...

SO THIS IS OUR HERO! A BIT ON THE SKINNY SIDE. BUT I'M STILL SURPRISED YOU DID SO WELL, FOR A MAN. COME CLOSER SO I MAY EMBRACE YOU!!

38B

SIT HERE NEXT TO ME! NO ONE WILL COME DISTURB US; LET'S MAKE THE BEST OF IT...

ER... YOU KNOW, I...

... AND TALK. WHERE DID YOU ACQUIRE SUCH PRODIGIOUS KNOWLEDGE OF WAR? USUALLY, ONLY WOMEN KNOW HOW TO FIGHT!

YOU SEE, YOUR MAJESTY, I'M NOT LIKE OTHER MEN. WHEN IT COMES TO WEAPONS, AS A MATTER OF FACT...

39A

... I HAVE A FEW THINGS HERE THAT YOU MIGHT FIND INTERESTING. LIKE THIS, FOR EXAMPLE...

WHAT IS IT?

A LIGHT STUNNER.

A STUNNER?
HOW DOES IT WORK?

... LIKE THIS. SORRY, MY GOOD WOMAN...

... BUT FOR THE QUEEN OF THE AMAZONS I FIND YOU RATHER CARELESS. NOW I'VE GOT TO CARRY THIS DEAD WEIGHT TO A SHIP. NOT AN EASY JOB...

PHEW... NOT AN EASY JOB AT ALL... I'M LUCKY, THOUGH. THIS PART OF THE PALACE SEEMS DESERTED.

39B

THE ROYAL FLAGSHIP! IF ONLY... **RATS!** GUARDS! QUICK, MY STUNNER!

WHO GOES THERE?

AND...

OK, ALL ABOARD! THERE'S NOT A MINUTE TO LOSE NOW; I DON'T WANT EVERY VIRAGO IN MALKA AFTER ME!

HEADING TO THE SKIFF. I'LL CALL LAURELINE ON THE WAY...

AT THAT MOMENT IN VALSENNAR...

THERE, DONE! ONE SLEEPING PILL IN THAT ARISTOCRATIC ALCOHOLIC'S CUP...

... AND I CAN GO. I'LL CALL VALERIAN AND TELL HIM I DID IT.

IN THE TROUBLED, STUFFY NIGHT OF ZAHIR, LAURELINE'S FLYER IS SOON ON ITS WAY TO THE CANYON, LIKE THAT OF VALERIAN, WHO HAS JUST RADIOED HER...

LAURELINE? IT WORKED FOR ME, I'M HEADING FOR THE SKIFF. WHAT'S YOUR STATUS?

MISSION ACCOMPLISHED. I'M ON MY WAY TOO!

A FEW HOURS LATER...

SO. THE SKIFF IS READY. KLOPKA'S STARTING TO STIR... AND HERE COMES LAURELINE!

MAY I INTRODUCE EMPEROR ALZAFRAR? HE'S STILL A BIT SLEEPY, BUT HE'LL BE ALL RIGHT.

AND THIS IS QUEEN KLOPKA. SLIGHTLY GROGGY BUT ALREADY AWAKE... COME THIS WAY NOW SO I CAN EXPLAIN...

THE SITUATION IS DIRE! WHILE I WAS WAITING FOR YOU, I TOOK A FEW SENSOR READINGS. YESTERDAY'S BATTLE HAS THROWN ZAHIR OFF COURSE FOR GOOD. IT'S NOW WITHIN THE GRAVITATIONAL WELL OF UKBAR'S STAR. WE ONLY HAVE A FEW DAYS TO ACT...

WHAT DO YOU INTEND TO DO?

WE'RE GOING TO NEED THE ZAHIRIANS' COLLABORATION. BUT FIRST, THEY HAVE TO UNDERSTAND WHAT THE UNIVERSE IS! SO, FIRST OF ALL, WE TAKE THEM TO SEE THE STARS. THEN...

WHAT...

PAK
OW

WHOA! WHOA! NOW'S NOT THE TIME!!

IT'S THAT SHREW! SHE ATTACKED ME WITHOUT WARNING!!!

THIS JACKANAPES SPLASHES HIMSELF WITH FLOWER ALCOHOL... TO WAKE HIMSELF UP, HE SAYS!! BLARGH! THE STINK...

ENOUGH! GIVE ME THIS VIAL AND GET IN THERE... YOUR MAJESTY!

YOU TOO, MY QUEEN! I HAVE SOMETHING TO SHOW YOU.

MOVE, YOU NINCOMPOOP!

YOU'RE SMOTHERING MEARRRGH...

FOR CRYING OUT LOUD! STOP FIGHTING FOR A MINUTE AND LOOK!

42 A

WE'RE NOW PASSING THROUGH ZAHIR'S OUTER SHELL.

AND THIS IS THE SKY. THE UNIVERSE, THE COSMOS...

42 B

I DON'T UNDERSTAND! WHERE ARE WE? WHAT ARE ALL THOSE LITTLE LIGHTS DOING UP THERE?

PFFF! YOU IDIOT... CAN'T YOU SEE THESE ARE PFITZ STONES SEWN ONTO AN ENORMOUS BLANKET OF BLACK FUFUNIL FABRIC! IT'S OBVIOUS, REALLY.

ERM... I DON'T MEAN TO CONTRADICT YOU, YOUR MAJESTY, BUT THAT'S NOT EXACTLY IT. AROUND US IS THE VOID. AND EACH OF THOSE LITTLE LIGHTS IS A SUN, NEXT TO WHICH ARE OTHER WORLDS LIKE ZAHIR...

THE V... V... VOID?!

OTHER ZAHIRS!? IMPOSSSSSS...

WHAT HAPPENED?

THE POOR DEARS PASSED OUT!

BOOM BOOM

YOU HAVE TO ADMIT, IT MUST BE QUITE A SHOCK FOR THE INHABITANTS OF A CLOSED WORLD TO DISCOVER THE STARS... WE'RE GOING TO HAVE TO GIVE THEM INTENSIVE HYPNO-EDUCATION.

GOT IT. HEADING FOR THE SHIP!

LATER, IN THE LARGE TERRAN SHIP'S HYPNO-LIBRARY, AFTER A LONG SESSION OF FORCED MEMORISATION UNDER HYPNOSIS...

SO THAT'S WHAT THE UNIVERSE IS! OH, MY HEAD HURTS...

WIMP! I UNDERSTOOD EVERYTHING EASILY!

OK. LISTEN TO ME, BOTH OF YOU... YOU NOW KNOW THAT ZAHIR IS DOOMED IF WE DON'T ACT IMMEDIATELY! I THINK I'VE FOUND A WAY TO STOP YOUR WORLD'S HEADLONG PLUNGE. TO DO THAT...

... I NEED YOUR WHOLE STOCK OF FLOGUMS. EVERY SINGLE ONE, YOU HEAR?!! THE LEMM PEOPLE, WHO ARE SKILLED IN THEIR HANDLING, WILL HAVE TO ASSIST YOU, AND MY FRIEND LAURELINE WILL BRING THEM HERE. CAN I COUNT ON YOUR HELP?...

YOU CAN, EARTHLING!

PERFECT, THEN! YOU'RE GOING TO GO BACK TO YOUR RESPECTIVE CITIES. THE SLIGHTEST DELAY WOULD DOOM US ALL AND WOULD ALSO MEAN DEATH FOR ALL THE COLONISTS OF UKBAR WHOSE EXISTENCE YOU JUST DISCOVERED...

44A

A SCANT FEW HOURS HAVE PASSED WHEN A DESPERATE ACTIVITY FILLS ZAHIR OF THE BURNING SUN, THE STRANGE LAND WITHOUT STARS...

EVERYWHERE, AS IF BY A MIRACLE, THE LOOMING DANGER ERASES THE WEIGHT OF THE UNMOVING PAST. IN MALKA, IN VALSENNAR AND AMONG THE LEMM PEOPLE...

... THE ZAHIRIANS, UNITED FOR THE FIRST TIME, MEN AND WOMEN WORKING SIDE BY SIDE, STRUGGLE TO SAVE THEIR PLANET IN DISTRESS.

44B

AND, WHILE VALERIAN IS LOST IN COMPLEX CALCULATIONS...

... LAURELINE TRANSPORTS FLOGUMS TO THE SHIP BY THE HUNDREDS...

FINALLY...

IT'S DONE, VALERIAN. EVERY FLOGUM WE COULD LAY OUR HANDS ON HAS BEEN BROUGHT TO THE MAGAZINE, AND THEIR AUTOMATIC DEPLOYMENT HAS BEEN PROGRAMMED ACCORDING TO YOUR NUMBERS.

I'M DONE HERE AS WELL.

WILL YOU FINALLY TELL ME WHAT YOU HAVE IN MIND?

YES. I'M GOING TO FIGHT FIRE WITH FIRE BY DROPPING FLOGUMS IN A CONCENTRIC PATTERN AROUND ZAHIR AND JUMPING THROUGH SPACE-TIME SO THEY EXPLODE SIMULTANEOUSLY! THAT WAY I SHOULD BE ABLE TO BREAK THE MOMENTUM OF THE PLANET AND SET IT ON A STABLE ORBIT AROUND UKBAR.

BUT... ZAHIR WILL BE TORN TO PIECES!

I DON'T THINK SO. I'VE WORKED IT ALL OUT: THE RISK OF EXPLOSION IN THE CORE, THE POSSIBILITY OF THE CRUST CRACKING ALONG THE GREAT CANYON, AND PLENTY MORE THINGS. IT SHOULD HOLD! THERE! THE JUMP IS SCHEDULED FOR THREE HOURS FROM NOW. YOU HAVE JUST ENOUGH TIME TO WARN OUR ZAHIRIAN FRIENDS.

A TIME OF UNBEARABLE FEAR BEGINS INSIDE ZAHIR...

READY, LAURELINE?
NOW!

... AS WELL AS ON THE PLANETS OF UKBAR, IN CONSTANT VIDEO CONTACT WITH THE SHIP. SUDDENLY...

... WITH A PRODIGIOUS WHITE FLASH, THE ENTIRE PLANET SEEMS TO STRETCH AND TWIST, LIKE DOUGH WHIPPED BY THE STRING OF EXPLOSIVES VALERIAN HAS WOVEN AROUND IT.

MUCH LATER...

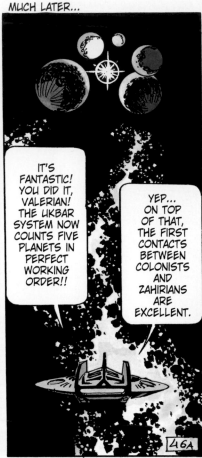

IT'S FANTASTIC! YOU DID IT, VALERIAN! THE UKBAR SYSTEM NOW COUNTS FIVE PLANETS IN PERFECT WORKING ORDER!!

YEP... ON TOP OF THAT, THE FIRST CONTACTS BETWEEN COLONISTS AND ZAHIRIANS ARE EXCELLENT.

YOU KNOW WHAT ELSE I HEARD? ZAHIR'S WHOLE SOCIETY IS COLLAPSING. THERE'S A VERITABLE EPIDEMIC OF MARRIAGES! THEY EVEN SAY THAT QUEEN KLOPKA HAS DECIDED TO MARRY EMPEROR ALZAFRAR!!! THE POOR MAN IS GOING TO DROWN IN FLOWER ALCOHOL FOR GOOD...

SPEAKING OF WHICH... WHAT ARE YOU DOING? THIS SMELL...

ME?... HIC... NOTHING! I'VE FINALLY FOUND THE TIME TO... SAMPLE ZAHIRIAN PRODUCTS... ANYWAY, I'VE BEEN THINKING... I'VE GOT NOTHING AGAINST MATRIARCHY... SEE? I'M LETTING YOU BRING US BACK TO GALAXITY!... AND BE QUICK ABOUT IT!

P. CHRISTIN J.C. MEZIERES

THE END

74

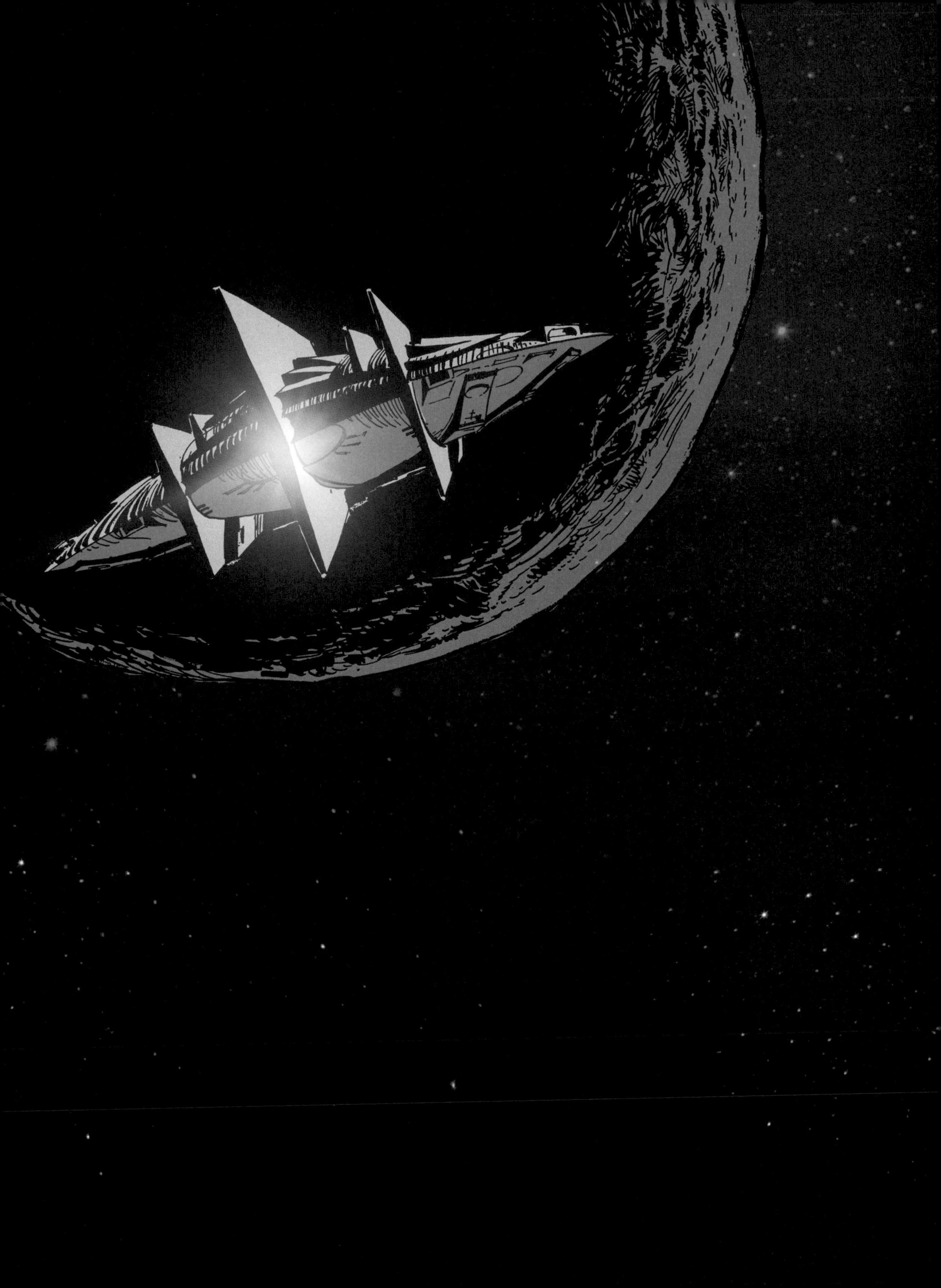

WELCOME TO ALFLOLOL

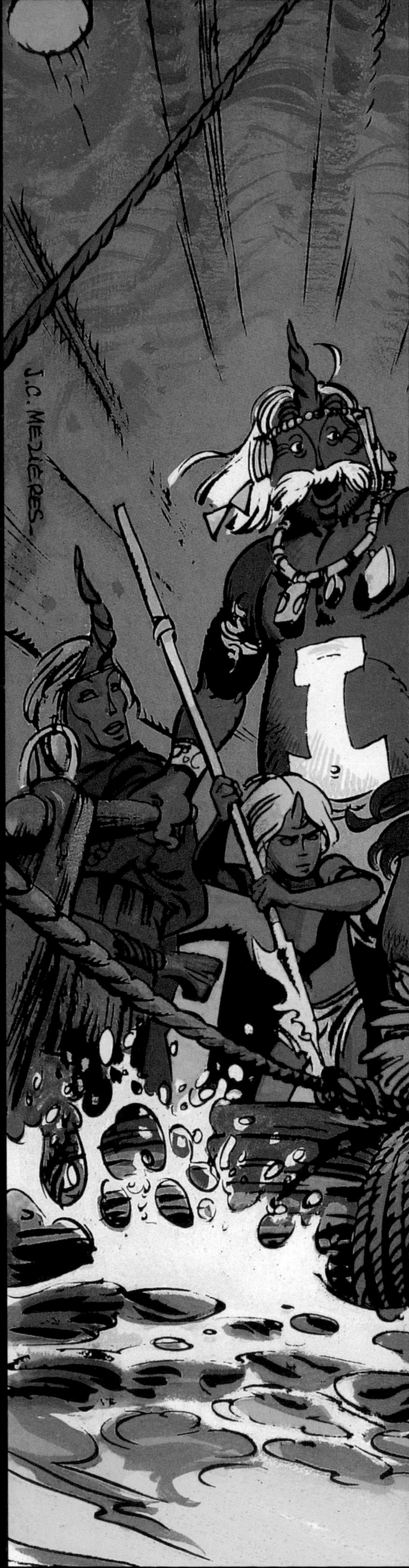
J.C. MEZIERES

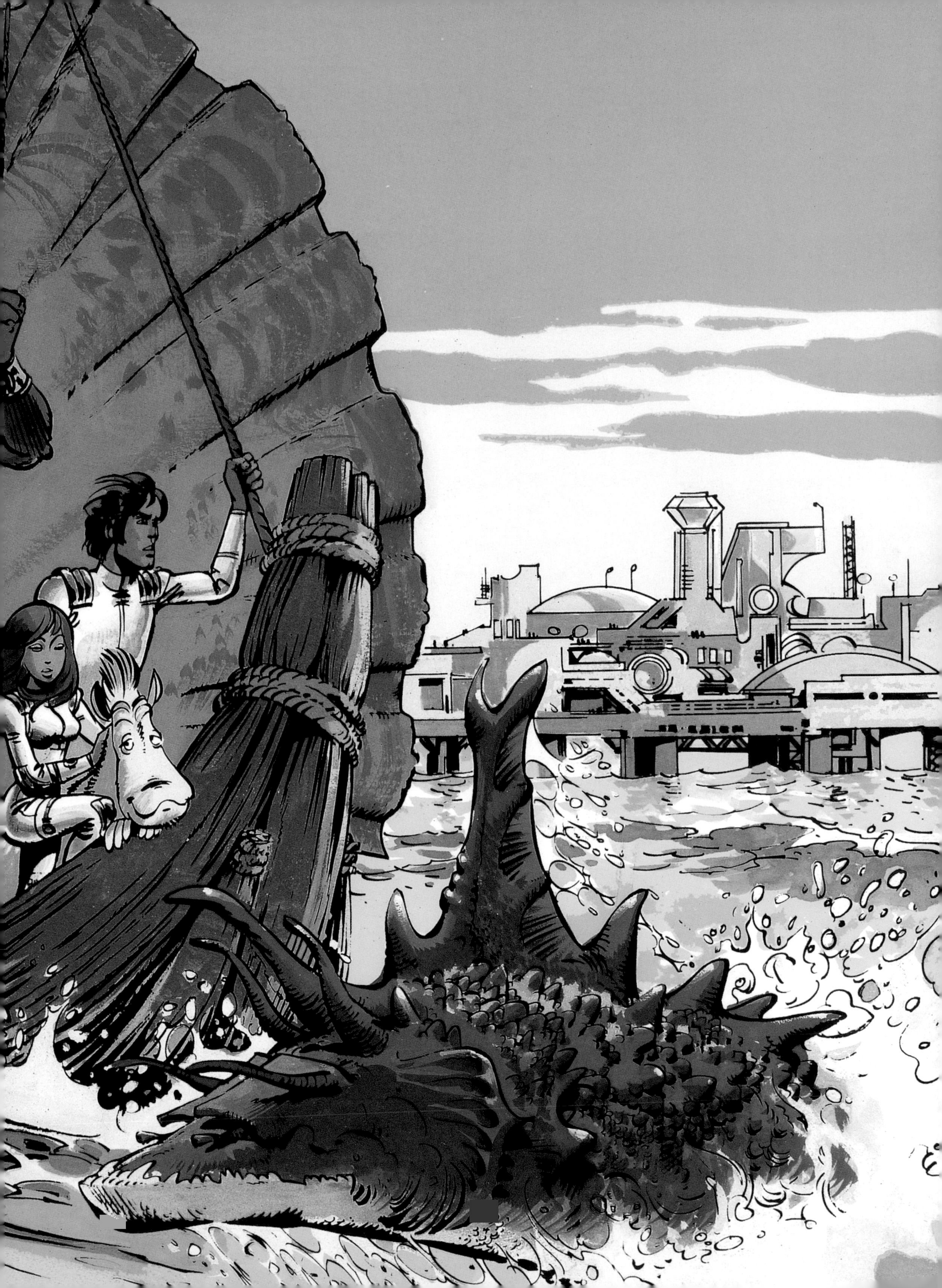

TECHNOROG! A MASSIVE PLANET WITH
INEXHAUSTIBLE RESOURCES. ONE OF THE
TERRAN GALACTIC EMPIRE'S VITAL STRATEGIC
POINTS. FROM ITS MOUNTAINS ARE MINED
THE RARE METALS NEEDED TO BUILD THE
EMPIRE'S SPACESHIPS. FROM ITS OCEANS
ARE GATHERED THE MAGNETIC SALTS THAT
FUEL THEIR FASTER-THAN-LIGHT ENGINES.
FROM ITS FACTORIES COME ENDLESS LINES
OF HEAVY EQUIPMENT BOUND FOR THE
OTHER PLANETS CONTROLLED BY EARTH.

TECHNOROG! A HARSH CLIMATE THAT OFTEN
SPAWNS THE MERCILESS DESERT SIROCCO,
BUT ALSO WONDERFUL FORESTS, STRANGE
MULTICOLOURED OCEANS AND IMPOSING
MOUNTAINS.
HUMANS HAVE SETTLED THIS PLANET—
UNINHABITED EXCEPT FOR SEVERAL GIGANTIC
ANIMAL SPECIES, HARMLESS PROVIDED THEY
ARE LEFT ALONE, FORTUNATELY—WITH
INTENSIVE EXPLOITATION IN MIND. PROTECTED
BY EARTH'S IMPOSING TECHNOLOGICAL
APPARATUS, SHELTERED INSIDE DOMES THAT
REPRODUCE THE CYCLE OF DAY AND NIGHT,
THEY KNOW NOTHING OF THE WORLD
AROUND THEM, OF THE SLOW RHYTHM OF
LIGHT AND DARKNESS, WHICH, EVERY 30
EARTH DAYS, RETURNS THE PLANET TO A
NIGHT THAT LASTS A FULL MOON.

THEY SET THEMSELVES AS ABSOLUTE MASTERS
OF THIS LAND THEY STRIP BARE, AND THEY
WORK... THE COLONISATION, ALREADY TWO
CENTURIES OLD BY NOW, HAS NEVER MET
WITH THE SLIGHTEST OBSTACLE. AND THE
FEW RELICS OF AN ANCIENT RACE, APPARENTLY
EXTINCT FOR SEVERAL MILLENNIA, HAVE
BEEN CARRIED OFF TO GALAXITY'S MUSEUM
OF SPACE, FAR AWAY TO DISTANT EARTH...

THIS IS THE WORLD THAT ONE OF THE SPATIO-
TEMPORAL SERVICE'S SPACESHIPS IS NOW
LEAVING BEHIND, APPROACHING THE ASTEROID
BELT ENCIRCLING TECHNOROG...

... AT THE CONTROLS ARE VALERIAN AND
LAURELINE, TWO YOUNG AGENTS OF THE
SERVICE, WHO ARE ON THEIR WAY BACK
TO EARTH AFTER AN INSPECTION TOUR OF
TECHNOROG.

UGHHH!... I CAN'T SAY I'M SAD TO LEAVE THAT PLACE! THOSE GUYS DOWN THERE—THEY'RE ALL SO GLUM!... IT'S JUST NOT RIGHT TO LOVE WORK THAT MUCH!

YOU'RE BEING UNFAIR, LAURELINE! TECHNOROG HAS THE BEST ENGINEERS AND TECHNICIANS IN THE EMPIRE. AND IF IT WEREN'T FOR THEM, YOU WOULDN'T BE SITTING COMFORTABLY IN YOUR CHAIR, READY TO MAKE THE BIG JUMP BACK TO GALAXITY WITHOUT HAVING TO LIFT A FINGER!...

BESIDES, THEY'RE ALL VOLUNTEERS. TECHNOROG IS THE FLAGSHIP OF EARTH'S INDUSTRY, AND...

OH, CAN IT! SAVE THE RAH-RAH SONG FOR YOUR INSPECTION REPORT. YOU'D BETTER KEEP YOUR EYES ON ALL THOSE ROCKS WE HAVE TO NAVIGATE!

HMM... YOU'RE PROBABLY RIGHT. WE'RE GETTING CLOSE TO THE REEFS. I'M GOING TO ASK FOR THE PROTECTIVE SHIELD TO BE OPENED.

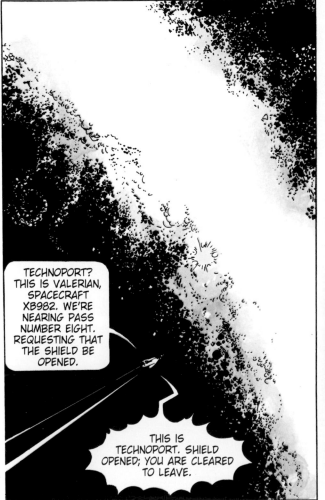

TECHNOPORT? THIS IS VALERIAN, SPACECRAFT XB982. WE'RE NEARING PASS NUMBER EIGHT. REQUESTING THAT THE SHIELD BE OPENED.

THIS IS TECHNOPORT. SHIELD OPENED; YOU ARE CLEARED TO LEAVE.

CAREFULLY MANOEUVRING BETWEEN THE REEFS, WEAVING TO FOLLOW THE CHANNEL MARKED BY THE ELECTROMAGNETIC BEACONS THAT SURROUND TECHNOROG IN AN UNBREACHABLE PROTECTIVE BUBBLE...

... VALERIAN TAKES HIS SPACECRAFT TOWARDS OPEN SPACE WHILE THE PASSAGE, TEMPORARILY OPENED, CLOSES BEHIND HIM.

OK. SPATIO-TEMPORAL COORDINATES ARE SET. WE CAN JUMP TO EARTH NOW. READY, LAURELINE?

LAURELINE

MY LITTLE LAURELINE! WHAT HAPPENED?

VALERIAN! IT'S... IT WAS STRANGE: I FELT SOMETHING LIKE A CALL, A CRY OF DESPAIR...

THERE'S SOMETHING OR SOMEONE NEAR US. AND IT... WHATEVER IT IS NEEDS OUR HELP... I FELT IT!

BY SPACE! IF THERE'S REALLY SOMETHING, WE OUGHT TO BE ABLE TO DETECT IT. YOU GO WATCH THE SENSOR SCREENS WHILE I TAKE US ALONG THE SHIELD...

WHILE VALERIAN SLOWLY GUIDES THE SHIP THROUGH CLUSTERS OF ROCKS...

... LAURELINE STRIVES TO LOCATE THE SOURCE OF THE STRANGE CALL.

SHE SCANS THE VOID IN VAIN FOR ENDLESS MINUTES, UNTIL...

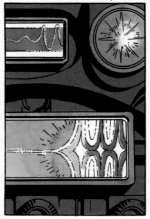

VALERIAN! THERE! THERE'S SOMETHING STRAIGHT AHEAD!

ON MY WAY!

WHAT A WEIRD STRUCTURE!!

IT'S A SHIP-ADRIFT. LOOK, IT'S FALLING TOWARDS THE PROTECTIVE SHIELD!!!

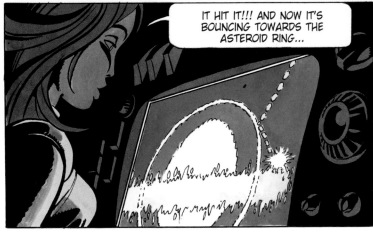

IT HIT IT!!! AND NOW IT'S BOUNCING TOWARDS THE ASTEROID RING...

YES... EVEN I CAN'T GO ANY FURTHER. IT'S TOO DANGEROUS!

THAT'S IT... IT'S RUN AGROUND!

AND THE SAME THING WILL HAPPEN TO US IF I GO ON. WE'LL PARK HERE IN ORBIT AND GO CHECK THE WRECK ON FOOT.

THE WEIRD THING IS, THERE HAVEN'T BEEN ANY OTHER CALLS. DO YOU THINK THAT THE... ER... PEOPLE ON THE SHIP DIED IN THE COLLISION?

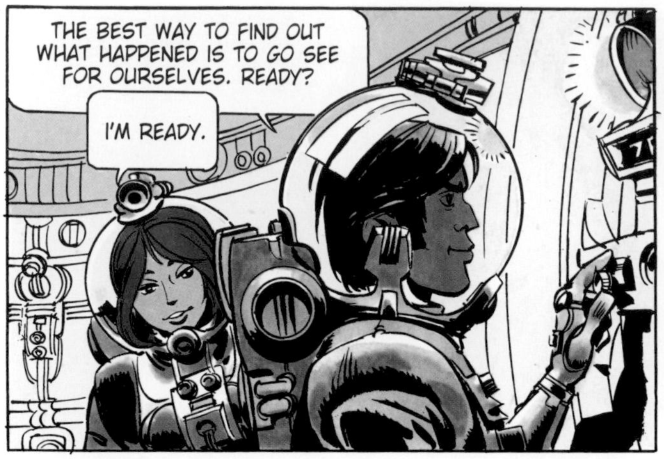
THE BEST WAY TO FIND OUT WHAT HAPPENED IS TO GO SEE FOR OURSELVES. READY?
I'M READY.

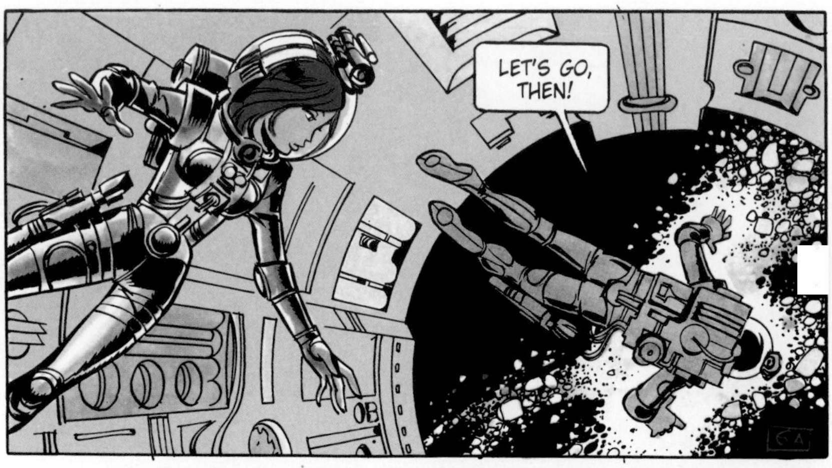
LET'S GO, THEN!

LEAVING THEIR SPACECRAFT, VALERIAN AND LAURELINE FLOAT LIGHTLY THROUGH THE ETHER AND, SLIPPING THROUGH THE TANGLE OF ROCKS...

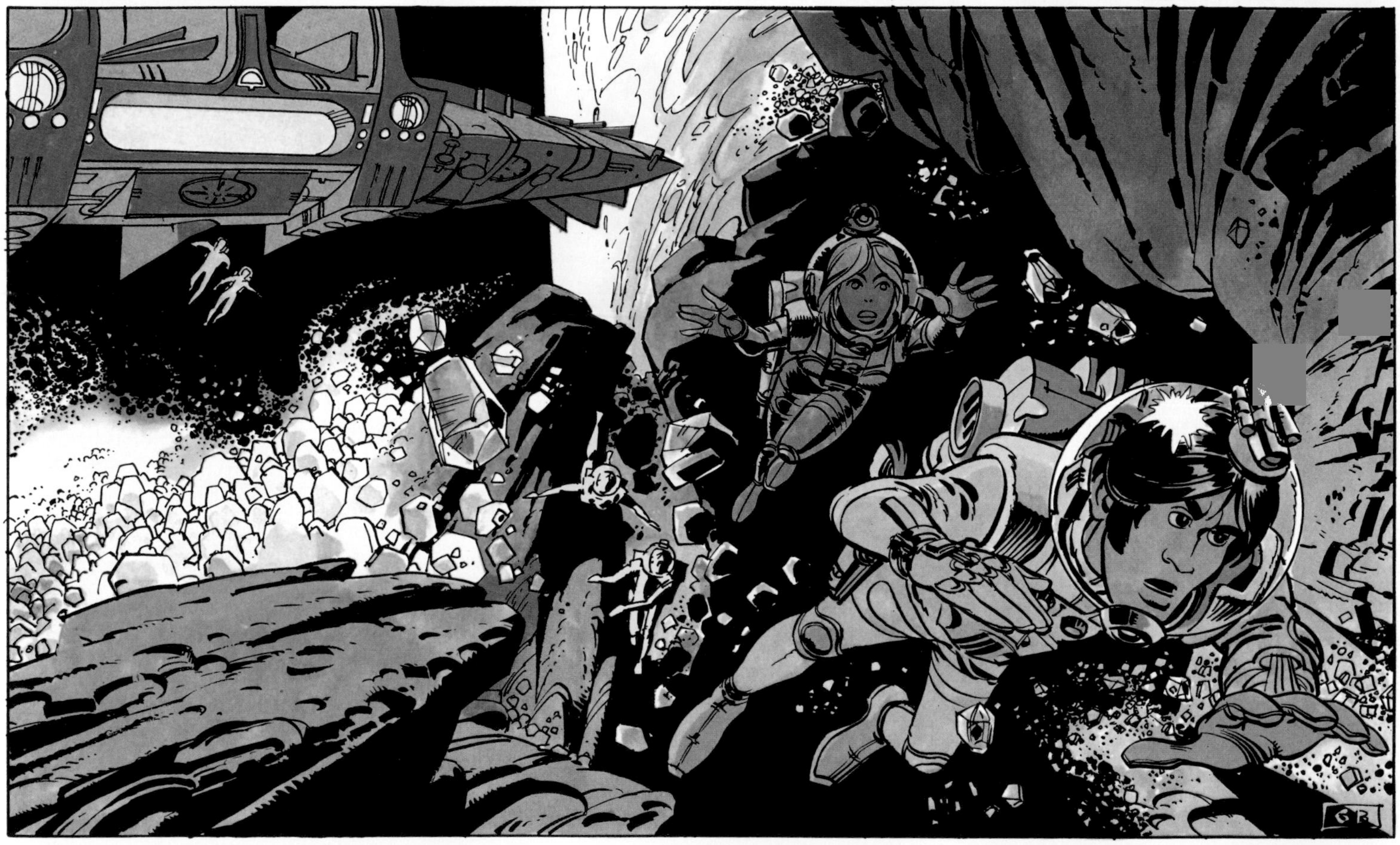

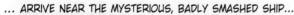

... ARRIVE NEAR THE MYSTERIOUS, BADLY SMASHED SHIP...

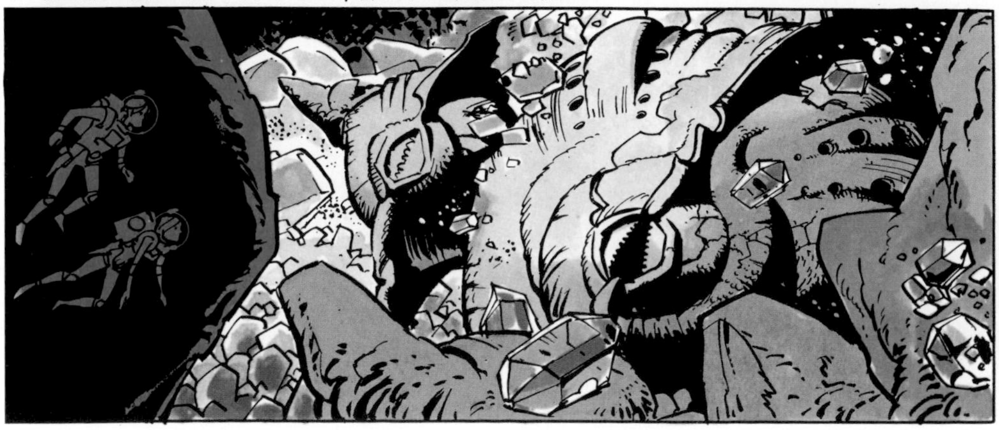

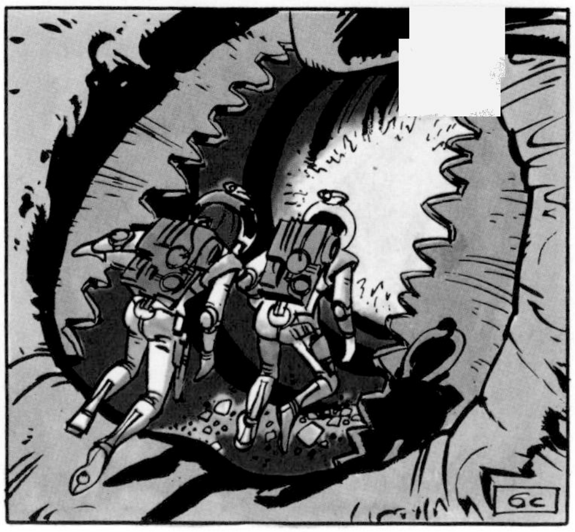

UP THERE MUST HAVE BEEN THE COCKPIT.

AND HERE WERE THE CREW'S LIVING QUARTERS... BUT IT'S ALL EMPTY.

HMM... ONE THING'S FOR SURE: THEY'RE NOT HUMAN! AS EVERYTHING IS OPEN TO SPACE, THEY MUST NOT NEED OXYGEN TO LIVE... AND, JUDGING BY THE SIZE OF THESE OBJECTS, THESE BEINGS MUST BE HUGE.

YES... AND THEY MUST HAVE QUITE THE APPETITE, TOO. COME SEE THIS!

THEIR FOOD STORES!

EMPTY AS WELL... THEY HAD NOTHING LEFT TO EAT! MAYBE THAT'S WHY THEY TRIED TO APPROACH TECHNOROG. WHAT DO YOU THINK, LAURELINE?

LAU...

OH, COME ON! NOT AGAIN! THAT GIRL HAS A KNACK FOR PUTTING HERSELF IN THE MOST RIDICULOUS SITUATIONS! WAIT A MINUTE...

NOW SHE'S FLOATING AWAY! LAURELINE!!!

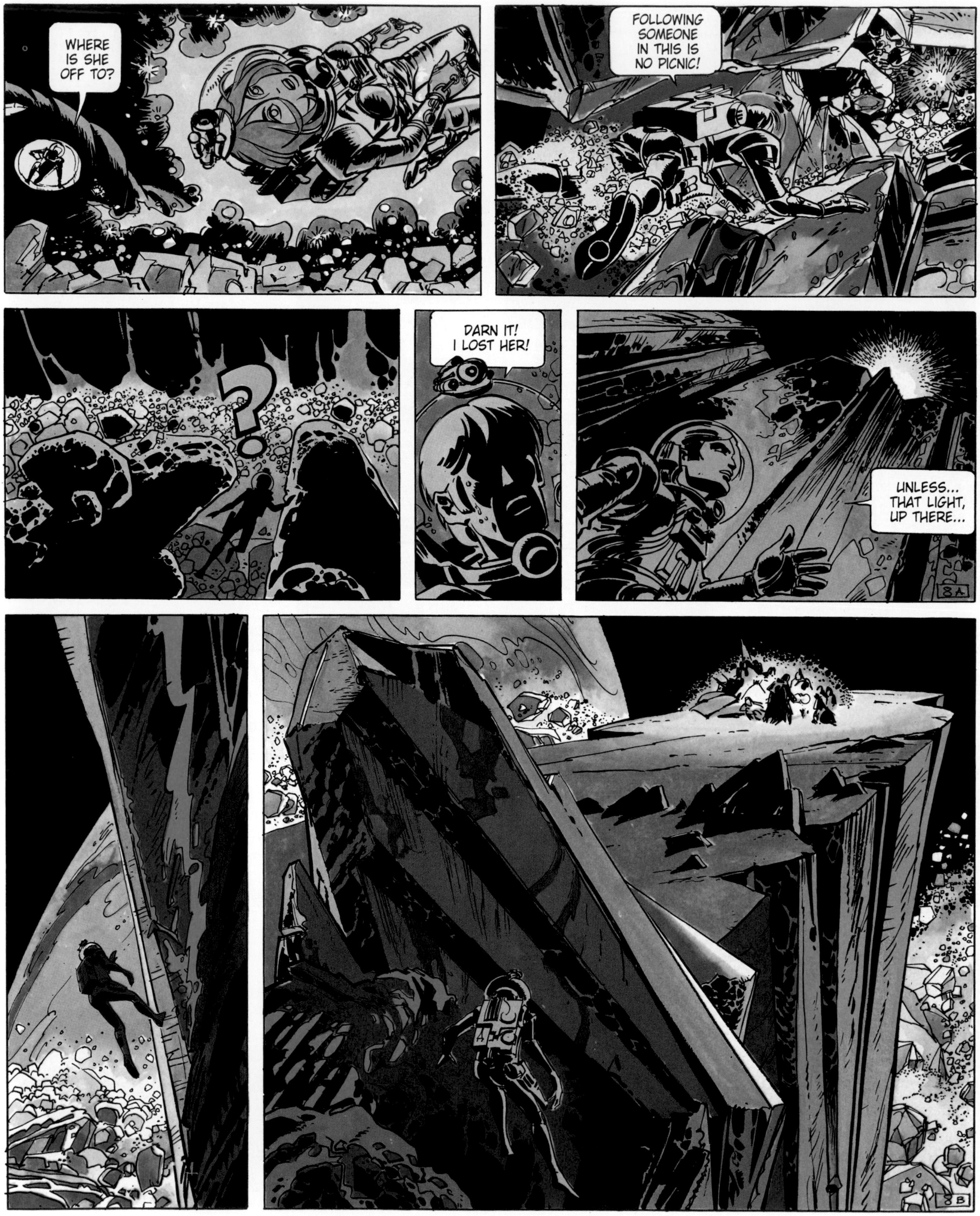
WHERE IS SHE OFF TO?
FOLLOWING SOMEONE IN THIS IS NO PICNIC!
DARN IT! I LOST HER!
UNLESS... THAT LIGHT, UP THERE...
8A
8B

NO DOUBT ABOUT IT: THESE ARE THE PEOPLE FROM THE SHIP. BUT...

CAN YOU NOT WAKE UP, LITTLE BEING? I CAN FEEL YOUR MIND, ALIVE BUT CAPTIVE...

... I DON'T BELIEVE IT... IT'S THAT GIANT I'M HEARING TALK TO LAURELINE!! A TELEPATH!!!

I AM GOING TO BREAK THIS SHELL TO TRY AND BRING YOU BACK TO YOUR SENSES. I CANNOT HELP YOU WHILE YOU ARE INSIDE YOUR SHELL...

OH, NO! IT'S LAURELINE'S SPACESUIT HE WANTS TO...

DON'T TOUCH ANYTHING!

WATCH IT! THIS IS A DEADLY WEAPON!

AH! IT DID SEEM TO ME WE FELT A SECOND MIND! REMAIN CALM, FRIEND...

WE WISH NO HARM TO THE OTHER LITTLE BEING. ON THE CONTRARY! WE KNOW SHE CAME TO HELP US...

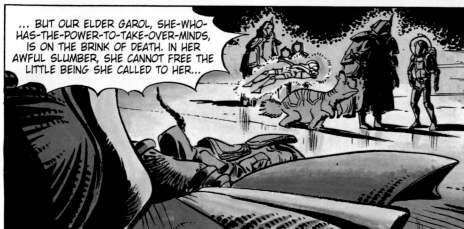

... BUT OUR ELDER GAROL, SHE-WHO-HAS-THE-POWER-TO-TAKE-OVER-MINDS, IS ON THE BRINK OF DEATH. IN HER AWFUL SLUMBER, SHE CANNOT FREE THE LITTLE BEING SHE CALLED TO HER...

IS THIS GAROL?... SHE LOOKS SERIOUSLY INJURED...

YES! SHE WAS HIT BY ROCKS WHEN OUR GREAT SHIP FLOUNDERED, AND...

I MAY BE ABLE TO SAVE HER IF YOU TAKE US BACK TO MY SHIP. BUT HOW CAN WE...

MY WIFE, ORGAL, HAS THE GIFT-OF-MAKING-THINGS-MOVE-THROUGH-SPACE. IT WAS SHE WHO PROPELLED OUR VESSEL. PERHAPS SHE CAN TAKE US ALL TO YOURS.

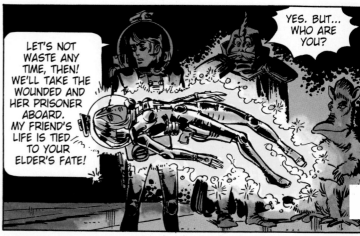

LET'S NOT WASTE ANY TIME, THEN! WE'LL TAKE THE WOUNDED AND HER PRISONER ABOARD. MY FRIEND'S LIFE IS TIED TO YOUR ELDER'S FATE!

YES. BUT... WHO ARE YOU?

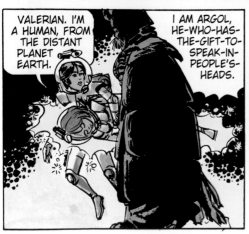

VALERIAN. I'M A HUMAN, FROM THE DISTANT PLANET EARTH.

I AM ARGOL, HE-WHO-HAS-THE-GIFT-TO-SPEAK-IN-PEOPLE'S-HEADS.

I SHALL TRANSLATE FOR YOU THE WORDS OF MY WHOLE FAMILY. THESE TWO ARE MY CHILDREN—THEY HAVE NOT YET DISCOVERED THEIR GIFTS...

... AND THE ANIMAL IS OUR FAMILY GUMUN. IT WAS HE WHO FELT YOUR PRESENCE!...

MAY WE GO? WE NEED TO HEAD THIS WAY TO...

SHHHH... BE SILENT NOW, FRIEND. ORGAL NEEDS ALL OF HER STRENGTH TO MAKE OUR OVERBURDENED SKIFF MOVE...

AND THEN, IN THE COLD SILENCE OF SPACE, A STUNNED VALERIAN LOOKS ON AS THE SMALL CRAFT RISES SLOWLY...

... AND, URGED ON SOLELY BY THE STRENGTH OF ORGAL'S INTENSE GAZE, FIXED UPON A MYSTERIOUS POINT AND PULSING WITH POWER...

... GENTLY MOVES TOWARDS HIS OWN SHIP.

THERE! YOU MAY SPEAK ANEW.

INCREDIBLE... IS THIS HOW YOUR BIG SHIP WORKED, TOO?

OF COURSE... THESE VESSELS WERE PULLED OUT OF THE SOIL OF OUR WORLD BY OUR ANCESTORS IN THE DAWN OF TIME. YOU CANNOT FIND THEM ANYMORE! BUT, WITH OURS, WE VISITED HUNDREDS OF WORLDS BEFORE WE CAME BACK TO CRASH HERE, ON ALFLOLOL...

WHAT DO YOU MEAN, ON ALFLOLOL?

WHAT—DO YOU NOT KNOW THE NAME OF THE WORLD YOU WERE COMING FROM? THIS WORLD IS OURS, AND IS NAMED ALFLOLOL.

NOT AT ALL! IT'S CALLED TECHNOROG, AND IT'S THE PLANET EARTH I TOLD YOU ABOUT THAT OCCUPIES IT...

HA! HA! YOU JEST! WHEN WE LEFT IT TO GO FOR A LITTLE TREK AMONG THE STARS, SOME 50,000 MOONS AGO, ITS NAME WAS ALFLOLOL! THEREFORE, THAT IS STILL ITS NAME, IS IT NOT?

TECHNOROG'S LUNAR MONTHS LAST 30 EARTH DAYS. SO, YOU MUST HAVE LEFT... UNNNH... **SOME 4,000 YEARS AGO!...** I THINK I'M STARTING TO UNDERSTAND...

YES. IT IS SIMPLE: WE ARE COMING HOME AFTER A LITTLE TRIP!

A LITTLE TRIP?! TELL ME, ARGOL, HOW LONG DO YOU LIVE?

OH, IT DEPENDS... OUR ELDER-FATHER PASSED AWAY WHEN WE BEGAN OUR TRIP. HE WAS ALMOST 300,000 MOONS OLD...

... OUR POOR ELDER-MOTHER, THOUGH, IS ONLY 220,000. WHICH IS MUCH TOO YOUNG TO DIE.

?!? YOUNG—AT OVER 17,000 YEARS OLD! WHAT ABOUT YOUR CHILDREN? HOW OLD ARE THEY?

LOGAR AND LAGOR? THEY ARE STILL YOUNG. THEY HAVE SEEN ONLY 42,000 AND 33,000 MOONS.

HMM... LITTLE SCAMPS OF A MERE 3,500 AND 2,500 YEARS... BY SPACE!

A LITTLE FARTHER...

ALL RIGHT. I'M GOING TO OPEN THE HOLD SO YOU CAN GO IN.

THE ELDER? HOW IS SHE?

SHE LIVES YET, BUT HER BODY IS DRYING UP MOST RAPIDLY...

AND YOU, MY POOR LAURELINE? WELL, IF YOU CAN HEAR ME: HAVE FAITH!

LEAVING THE SMALL SKIFF, VALERIAN ENTERS HIS OWN SHIP. AND, SHORTLY AFTERWARDS, ARGOL AND HIS FAMILY ARE ABOARD WITH HIM.

FOLLOW ME, QUICK! WE'RE GOING TO TAKE YOUR ELDER TO MY LABORATORY.

LABORATORY? I DO NOT UNDERSTAND, EARTHLING, BUT I TRUST YOU...

... SOME LONG MINUTES LATER...

I THINK I DID IT! THE DESICCATION HAS STOPPED...

SHE MOVED! I BELIEVE SHE HAS REGAINED CONSCIOUS-NESS...

BOOM

LAURELINE! MY SWEET LAURELINE!!!

"MY SWEET LAURELINE..." YAP YAP YAP... YOU'D GONE AND FORGOTTEN ME, HADN'T YOU?!...

BUT...

OH, DROP IT! FORTUNATELY, THERE ARE OTHERS HERE WHO LOVE ME MORE THAN YOU.

LAURELINE!!! I ASSURE YOU...

FRIEND, OUR ELDER THANKS YOU THROUGH MY VOICE! SHE FEELS MUCH BETTER. OUR FRIENDSHIP SHALL LAST FOREVER!

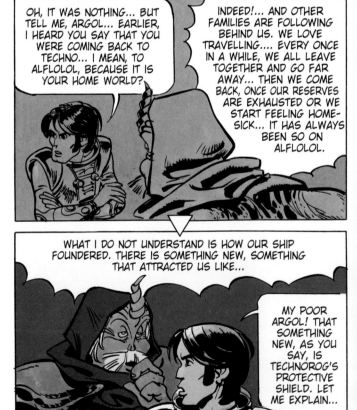

OH, IT WAS NOTHING... BUT TELL ME, ARGOL... EARLIER, I HEARD YOU SAY THAT YOU WERE COMING BACK TO TECHNO... I MEAN, TO ALFLOLOL, BECAUSE IT IS YOUR HOME WORLD?

INDEED!... AND OTHER FAMILIES ARE FOLLOWING BEHIND US. WE LOVE TRAVELLING.... EVERY ONCE IN A WHILE, WE ALL LEAVE TOGETHER AND GO FAR AWAY... THEN WE COME BACK, ONCE OUR RESERVES ARE EXHAUSTED OR WE START FEELING HOME- SICK... IT HAS ALWAYS BEEN SO ON ALFLOLOL.

WHAT I DO NOT UNDERSTAND IS HOW OUR SHIP FOUNDERED. THERE IS SOMETHING NEW, SOMETHING THAT ATTRACTED US LIKE...

MY POOR ARGOL! THAT SOMETHING NEW, AS YOU SAY, IS TECHNOROG'S PROTECTIVE SHIELD. LET ME EXPLAIN...

VALERIAN! CALL FROM TECHNOROG!! THEY'RE FURIOUS AND WANT TO KNOW WHY WE'RE STILL IN THE PROXIMITY OF THE PASSES! APPARENTLY, IT'S DANGEROUS...

HMM... THERE'S A DECISION TO BE MADE... CALL THE GOVERNOR- PRIORITY MESSAGE!

ARE YOU CERTAIN YOU WANT TO RETURN HOME, MY FRIENDS?

OF COURSE... WHY WOULD WE NOT, ANYWAY?...

THAT'S ALL I WANTED TO KNOW, THANKS...

I SURE HOPE YOU'RE GOING TO GIVE IT STRAIGHT TO THAT BUREAUCRAT! THOSE POOR PEOPLE CAN'T STAY LIKE THAT...

I'LL DO WHAT I CAN!

THE GOVERNOR WILL TAKE YOUR CALL NOW...

WELL, WHAT'S GOING ON?

DO YOU KNOW YOU ARE BREAKING REGULATIONS FOR...

GOVERNOR!!! SIR, I REQUEST CLEARANCE TO RETURN TO TECHNOPORT...

OH... ER... WELL, THEN, I SUPPOSE... CLEARANCE AND AUDIENCE GRANTED...

... I ALSO REQUEST AN AUDIENCE AS SOON AS I ARRIVE. THE SITUATION IS SERIOUS...

SOON, AFTER HAVING GONE THROUGH THE PASS AGAIN, VALERIAN'S SHIP IS FLYING LOW OVER TECHNOROG'S SURFACE, AT THE REQUEST OF ARGOL AND HIS FAMILY...

AS THEY GLIDE PAST THE MASSIVE FLOATING STATIONS OF MAGNETOCEAN...

... THE GIGANTIC MINES IN THE MOUNTAINS...

... THE COLOSSAL FACTORIES BUILT UPON THE PLAINS...

... AND THE PERFECTLY EVENLY SPACED HYDRO-PONIC PLANTATIONS...

... THE SHIP'S PASSENGERS ARE INCREASINGLY STUNNED...

WHAT... WHAT HAPPENED TO OUR WORLD? I DO NOT EVEN RECOGNISE IT ANYMORE...

THIS IS EARTH AND ITS CIVILISATION YOU'RE SEEING HERE, ARGOL.

AH!
THIS PLACE
I RECOGNISE...
IT IS THE FOREST
OF ANANIL,
THE BEAUTIFUL
FOREST NEAR
OUR CAMPSITE...

YOUR CAMPSITE?
WHERE IS IT LOCATED?

OVER
THERE, ON
THE LOVELY
HILL OF...

OOOOH!!
ALL THOSE THINGS
ON OUR HILL, ON
THE LAND OF OUR
ANCESTORS!!

THERE?!
THAT'S
TECHNO-
ROGRAD
!!

WHY ALL THOSE BIG...
ER... TRANSPARENT
TENTS?

BECAUSE HUMANS CANNOT LIVE
THE SAME WAY YOU DO. THEY FIND
THE LONG NIGHT-AND-DAY CYCLES
OF ALFLOLOL DIFFICULT TO HANDLE.

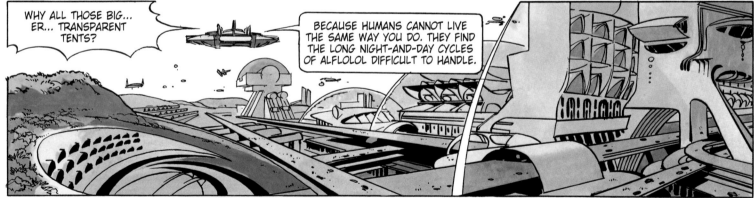

BUT WHY DID
THEY COME,
THEN?

TO WORK!!

I REALLY DO
NOT UNDER-
STAND!

YOU WILL
VERY SOON...

GET READY!
WE'RE ABOUT TO
LAND. I BELIEVE
SOME PEOPLE ARE
EAGER TO SEE US...

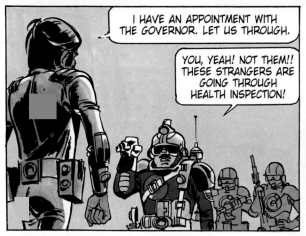

I HAVE AN APPOINTMENT WITH THE GOVERNOR. LET US THROUGH.

YOU, YEAH! NOT THEM!! THESE STRANGERS ARE GOING THROUGH HEALTH INSPECTION!

STRANGERS! US!! IT IS THEY WHO...

LET IT GO, MY FRIEND... DO AS THEY ASK. YOU'LL MAKE THINGS EASIER FOR ME.

AS FOR THAT ANIMAL THERE, HE GOES THROUGH THE SPACE CRITTER DOOR!!

OUR GUMUN !!!

I'LL GO WITH HIM AND JOIN YOU AFTER-WARDS...

WE HAVE A HOVERCAR WAITING FOR YOU, AGENT VALERIAN.

I'M GOING! I'M GOING!

AND WHILE VALERIAN ENTERS TECHNOROGRAD PROPER...

GO ON, MOVE IT, YOU FLEABAGS!!

INSIDE TECHNOROGRAD, IT'S THE USUAL SIGHTS...

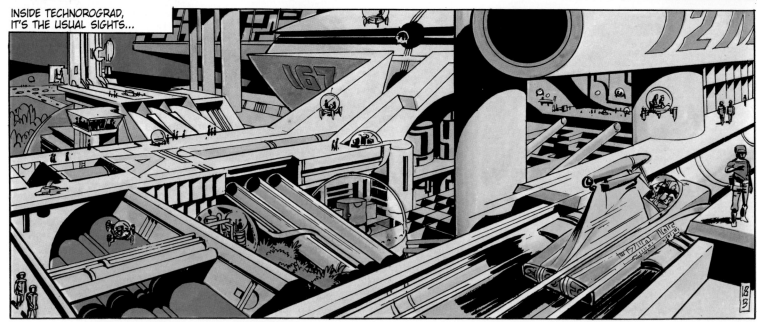

... WORKERS HEADING FOR THE MINES...

... COMING BACK FROM THE FACTORIES...

... GETTING READY FOR THE TRIP TO MAGNETOCEAN...

... OR RETURNING FROM THE HYDROPONIC FARMS.

WHEN VALERIAN LEAVES THE INDUSTRIAL DISTRICT FOR THE ENTERTAINMENT SECTOR, HE COMES IN SIGHT AT LAST OF THE ENORMOUS ADMINISTRATIVE BUILDING THAT, SITTING ATOP THE CENTRAL HILL, TOWERS ABOVE ALL OF TECHNOROGRAD.

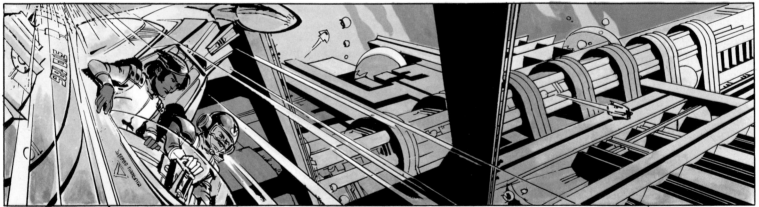

AND, IN FACT, A FEW MINUTES LATER, AT THE TOP OF THE MONUMENTAL STRUCTURE...

WELL, AGENT VALERIAN! MORE OF YOUR FANCIES, THEN?! WHY DID IT TAKE YOU SO LONG TO MAKE IT TO THE CITY? I'M WORRIED—AND I HAVE BETTER THINGS TO DO THAN WAIT FOR YOU!

AND YET, YOU'RE GOING TO HAVE TO LISTEN TO ME CAREFULLY. **THE NATIVE INHABITANTS OF TECHNOROG ARE BACK!!**

YOU'RE JOKING!! THIS PLANET HAS BEEN EMPTY OF INTELLIGENT LIFE FOR OVER 4,000 YEARS! TERRAN SCIENTISTS HAVE...

HA, HA! PRECISELY! THE ALFLOLOLIANS—THAT'S HOW THEY CALL THEMSELVES—JUST WENT FOR A LITTLE TRIP, THAT'S ALL! AND THE BONES AND ARTEFACTS RECOVERED BY OUR ARCHAEOLOGICAL TEAMS WERE THOSE OF THEIR ANCESTORS. BUT THEY ARE COMPLETELY ALIVE!

AND... HOW MANY ARE THERE?

IN MY SHIP, I BROUGHT BACK A FAMILY OF FIVE.

FIVE?... OH, GOOD, THEN, WE'LL SORT THIS OUT.

YOU THINK SO?... THERE ARE OTHER FAMILIES THAT WILL FOLLOW THIS ONE, SOONER OR LATER...

REALLY?... HMM. THIS IS ALL RATHER VEXING. JUST WHEN PRODUCTION WAS REALLY STARTING TO TAKE OFF, IT'S...

WELL, VEXING OR NOT, YOU KNOW THE GALACTIC CODE, I HOPE. IT WAS GALAXITY THAT DRAFTED IT, AFTER ALL, AND THAT'S ALL TO ITS CREDIT.

YES, OF COURSE... BUT THE CODE HAS NEVER BEEN APPLIED IN SUCH A SITUATION...

... IT'S THE FIRST TIME THAT A PLANET FULLY COLONISED BY EARTH HAS LATER BEEN DISCOVERED TO HAVE A NATIVE POPULATION, AND...

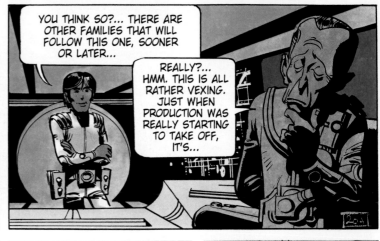

NOW, NOW! CALL GALAXITY IF YOU WANT, BUT THEY'LL TELL YOU THE SAME THING I DID. THE ALFLOLOLIANS HAVE THE RIGHT TO HAVE THEIR ANCESTRAL LANDS RETURNED TO THEM...

AND... ERM... DO THEY SEEM HOSTILE, THESE ALOF... AFLOL... WHAT DID YOU CALL THEM?

THE ALFLOLO-LIANS? NO, NOT AT ALL.

THAT'S WONDERFUL NEWS, MY DEAR VALERIAN. WE SHOULD BE ABLE TO NEGOTIATE, THEN, SHOULDN'T WE?...

WELL... THEY'RE NOT HOSTILE, BUT THEY'RE VERY BIG, VERY STRONG, VERY SMART, AND THEY HAVE SOME QUITE EXTRAORDINARY POWERS...

BIG, STRONG... LISTEN, VALERIAN, I CAN'T MAKE A DECISION WITHOUT CONVENING TECHNOROG'S COUNCIL FIRST...

THE COUNCIL!? BUT...

THEREFORE, I PROPOSE WE START BY PLACING YOUR AFLO... ALFLOLOLIANS IN QUARANTINE TO AVOID ANY CONTAMINATION. THEN...

I RAN THE MANDATORY TESTS WHEN I TREATED ONE OF THEM. THERE WERE NO MICROORGANISMS PRESENT!

TUT, TUT. QUARANTINE FIRST, I SAID. I'LL GIVE THE APPROPRIATE ORDERS TO... BUT WHAT IS THAT RACKET?!!

BOOM

BONK

US!

THEY WERE ANNOYING US WITH ALL THEIR CHECKPOINTS, SO WE CAME TO MEET YOU. I HOPE YOU'RE PLEASED?

I... I FORBID YOU...

ME? OH...

WUUUUUU

THE ALARMS! ALL OF THEM AT THE SAME TIME!!

INTERESTING PLACE, THIS IS. SAY, WHAT ARE ALL THESE LITTLE RED LAMPS THAT JUST LIT UP??

WHAT'S GOING ON??

THIS IS COMPLETE CHAOS!!

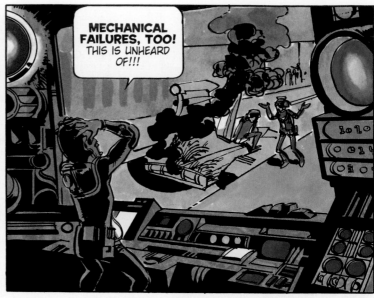

MECHANICAL FAILURES, TOO! THIS IS UNHEARD OF!!!

LAURE-LINE!

WELL, YES... THAT WAS US...

... WE'VE FOOLED ABOUT A LITTLE WITH THE GUMUN...

DO YOU HAVE ANY IDEA WHAT YOU'VE DONE, YOU SILLY GIRL?!

THESE THINGS ARE NOT VERY STURDY. WE DID NOT EVEN PLAY WITH THEM THAT LONG!

SO, YOU'RE THE ONES BREAKING MY CITY! OH, BUT IT'S GOING TO COST YOU! FIRST OFF, GET OUT OF HERE!!! OR MY GUARDS...

NO! WE ARE NOT GETTING OUT. WE WISH TO STAY! WE LIKE IT, AND WE HAVE THE RIGHT...

THAT TAKES THE CAKE! YOU...

HOLD ON, GOVERNOR. I THINK YOU MISUNDERSTAND. I EXPLAINED THEIR RIGHTS TO THE ALFLOLOLIANS. AND THE THING IS, ARGOL'S FAMILY LIVED IN THIS EXACT SPOT BEFORE THEY LEFT...

OF COURSE WE DID! THE LOVELIEST HILL ON ALFLOLOL. MY COMPLIMENTS, GOVERNOR. YOU CHOSE WELL.

HUH-UH... YOU'LL HAVE TO PROVE IT FIRST...

EASY. ALL YOU HAVE TO DO IS PULL DOWN YOUR BUILDING AND DIG DEEP ENOUGH...

YES. ALL OUR FAMILY'S GRAVES SINCE TIME IMMEMORIAL ARE BURIED UNDER THE HILL...

VALERIAN! YOU CAN'T LET THEM DO THIS!

ER... I'M AFRAID YOU HAVE LITTLE CHOICE BUT TO GIVE IN, GOVERNOR. THE GALACTIC CODE IS QUITE CLEAR...

AND, IN THE ARTIFICIAL EVENING, WHILE HARD-WORKING TECHNOROG SLEEPS UNDER ITS PROTECTIVE DOME, UNEXPECTED SOUNDS DRIFT DOWN FROM THE TOP OF THE ADMINISTRATIVE PALACE...

... WHERE, IN SHARP CONTRAST TO THE FUNCTIONAL COLDNESS OF THE PLACE, THE ALFLOLOLIANS HAVE SET UP THEIR CAMP.

AH, FRIENDS! HOW JOYOUS IT IS TO HAVE YOU WITH US! WE SHALL PROPERLY CELEBRATE OUR RETURN TO BEAUTIFUL ALFLOLOL!

CAREFUL, MY CHILDREN. DO NOT BREAK TOO MANY THINGS. THE EARTHLINGS ARE NOT LIKE US; THEY SEEM TO VALUE THEIR MATERIAL POSSESSIONS.

IF YOU CATCH ME, I'LL GIVE YOU A KISS!

CRACK

OH DEAR. VALERIAN'S GOING TO BE MAD AGAIN! THAT BOY'S SO SERIOUS...

SHE'S REALLY STARTING TO GET ON MY NERVES... AND I CAN'T TAKE THIS ANYMORE...

A FIVE-DAY PARTY. I'M BEAT...

AH, VALERIAN... YOU, TOO, ARE WANDERING THE CORRIDORS...

DON'T THOSE PEOPLE EVER SLEEP?

THEY DO... THEY DO... A FEW WINKS HERE AND THERE... THAT'S ENOUGH FOR THEM...

IS IT? WELL, I'M GOING TO GET SOME REST. THE WORST THING IS THAT I CAN'T GET ANY WORK DONE WITH ALL THAT...

WORK? OF COURSE, THE VERY NOTION IS INCOMPREHENSIBLE TO THEM. THEY HAVE NO IDEA WHY YOU'D WANT THEM TO LET YOU WORK.

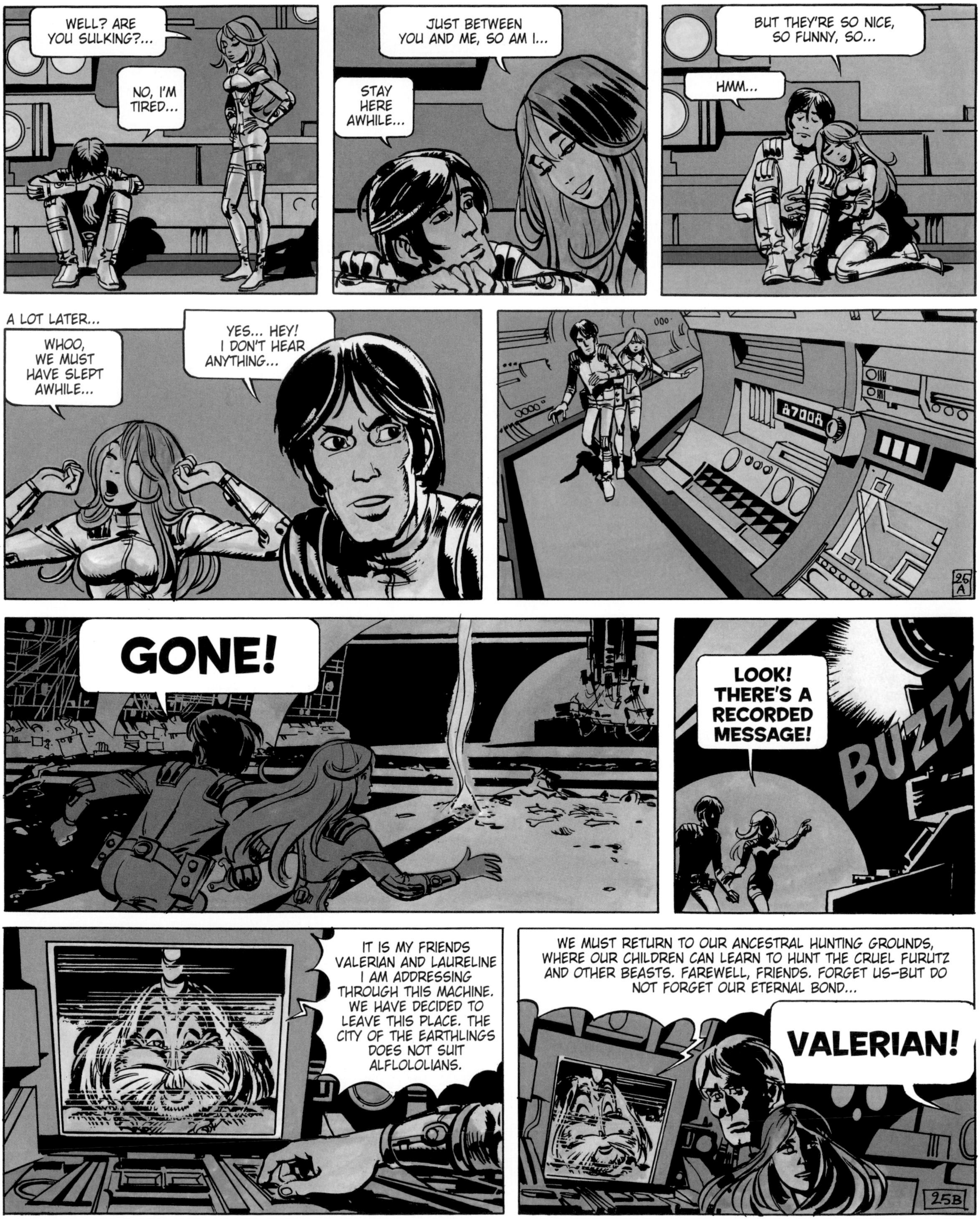

WELL? ARE YOU SULKING?...
NO, I'M TIRED...
JUST BETWEEN YOU AND ME, SO AM I...
STAY HERE AWHILE...
BUT THEY'RE SO NICE, SO FUNNY, SO...
HMM...
A LOT LATER...
WHOO, WE MUST HAVE SLEPT AWHILE...
YES... HEY! I DON'T HEAR ANYTHING...
25A
GONE!
LOOK! THERE'S A RECORDED MESSAGE!
BUZZ
IT IS MY FRIENDS VALERIAN AND LAURELINE I AM ADDRESSING THROUGH THIS MACHINE. WE HAVE DECIDED TO LEAVE THIS PLACE. THE CITY OF THE EARTHLINGS DOES NOT SUIT ALFLOLOLIANS.
WE MUST RETURN TO OUR ANCESTRAL HUNTING GROUNDS, WHERE OUR CHILDREN CAN LEARN TO HUNT THE CRUEL FURUTZ AND OTHER BEASTS. FAREWELL, FRIENDS. FORGET US–BUT DO NOT FORGET OUR ETERNAL BOND...
VALERIAN!
25B

... AND THE OTHER EARTHLINGS HAVE NOTHING TO FEAR. ALFLOLOLIANS ARE NOT A WAR-LIKE PEOPLE.

THE... THE STRANGE COMPANY YOU KEEP...

... HAS MADE A PROPER MESS AGAIN!!!

REALLY?

WE WERE IN A COUNCIL MEETING WHEN... HERE, JUST SEE FOR YOURSELVES...

OVER 1,000 GUARDS, POLICEMEN...

... RADAR TECHNICIANS, AND OTHERS...

... ALL CATALEPTIC! INCAPABLE OF TALKING OR MOVING!!!

PFFFF...

ERM! I SEE ELDER GAROL HAS RECOVERED FULLY... A THOUSAND AT THE SAME TIME!

NO MATTER WHAT, THIS SITUATION CANNOT GO ON! AS MINING MANAGER, I MUST PROTEST!

AND I, GENERAL DIRECTOR OF PRODUCTION FOR TECHNOROG'S FACTORIES, MUST OFFICIALLY WARN YOU!

CHAOS, MY YOUNG FRIENDS! CHAOS!!! WHAT COULD BE WORSE FOR PRODUCTION, I ASK YOU?

ALL OF THIS IS INTOLERABLE! AT LEAST, WHEN THEY WERE HERE, WE KNEW WHAT THEY WERE UP TO! WE MUST BRING THEM BACK! AN EXPEDITION IS READY...

YOU'RE CRAZY! YOUR BUSINESS IS OF NO INTEREST TO THEM. JUST LEAVE THEM ALONE...

YOUNG LADY, YOU ARE A SUBVERSIVE ELEMENT! YOU, VALERIAN, ON THE OTHER HAND, UNDERSTAND THAT TECHNOROG'S INDUSTRIAL POTENTIAL IS AT STAKE, DON'T YOU? TECHNOROG IS AN INDUSTRIAL PLANET, NOT A CAMP FOR TOURISTS AND ADVENTURERS. WHICH IS ALSO WHY WE LACK PEOPLE LIKE YOU AND WHY YOU'RE GOING TO LEAD THAT EXPEDITION...

ME?... ER, YOU KNOW...

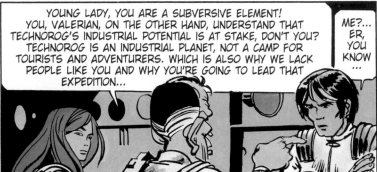

THEY HEADED FOR THE THICK FOREST THAT STANDS BETWEEN TECHNOROGRAD AND MAGNETOCEAN. BUT WE CAN'T DETECT THEM FROM THE AIR ANYMORE. WE'VE LOST CONTACT WITH THE PROBES.

THEREFORE, YOU MUST FIND THEM OVERLAND. THAT'S AN ORDER...

IN THAT CASE...

SIR, YES, SIR AND BY THE BOOK, HUH?!

OH, GIVE ME A BREAK! IT'S BETTER IF WE'RE THE ONES GOING AFTER THEM, DON'T YOU THINK?

HMM... MAYBE. BUT THAT FOREST IS THE ONE THAT ARGOL AND HIS FAMILY CALLED ANANIL. SOMETHING TELLS ME IT WON'T BE EASY TO FOLLOW THEM...

ALL RIGHT!

AH! I'M GLAD TO SEE YOU'RE COMING BACK TO YOUR SENSES. NO TIME TO WASTE, THEN...

AND SO, SOON...

BY THE WAY, YOUR ASSORTED GUARDS?

THEY CAME TO, BUT THEY HAVE NO MEMORY OF WHAT HAPPENED...

WE'VE ASSEMBLED THE MOST MODERN EQUIPMENT AND THE MOST QUALIFIED OFFICERS FOR YOUR EXPEDITION...

OH, YOU'RE TOO GOOD TO US!!! BAH... ENOUGH CHIT-CHAT. SINCE WE HAVE TO: **LET'S GO!**

MUCH LATER...

COME ON! GET A MOVE ON!

WE CAN'T START HER UP—THE MOSSES ATE EVERYTHING!!!

FURTHER...

THE LAST VEHICLE TOOK A WRONG TURN, AND...

KEEP GOING!

FURTHER STILL...

OW

DO SOME-THING!!!

OUR LAST ABLE MEN HAVE BEEN SNATCHED BY THAT CARNIVOROUS PLANT!!! WE HAVE TO FREE THEM AND GO BACK!

YOU'RE RIGHT...

ALL OF THE EQUIPMENT IS USELESS, AND YOUR MEN AREN'T MUCH BETTER! FREE THEM, AND SAY GOODBYE! **YOU** ARE GOING BACK...

BUT WE KEEP GOING, DON'T WE, VALERIAN?

YEAH, WE KEEP GOING!... WITH NOTHING BUT THIS RUBBISH DETECTOR AND A HOPELESSLY MUTE MICRO-RADIO THAT CAN'T PUNCH THROUGH THIS BLASTED JUNGLE...

COME ON! I'M SURE WE'LL FIND THEM!

THE JUNGLE GROWS STEADILY THICKER, AND, AFTER MANY LONG HOURS OF WALKING...

SO, THE DETECTOR?

IT'S GIVING OFF A FAINT SIGNAL, BUT IT COULD BE JUST ABOUT ANYTHING. THE TRAIL IS SO OLD...

BUT LOOK AT THE MAP! WE'VE CROSSED THE FOREST AT ITS NARROWEST POINT. I'M SURE THEY MUST HAVE FOLLOWED THE SAME PATH TO REACH MAGNETOCEAN...

NO DOUBT. WE'LL SEE. WE'RE VERY CLOSE TO THE SHORE NOW...

FIRST THINGS FIRST... WE SHOULD CAMP, SLEEP AND RECOVER SOME OF OUR STRENGTH. WE'VE BEEN WALKING ON OUR OWN FOR OVER 48 HOURS...

AS YOU WISH.

AND...

SUDDENLY...

VALERIAN! IT'S GOT ME!

UNBELIEVABLE! SHE'S GOING TO GET HERSELF CARRIED OFF BY SOME MONSTER AGAIN. THIS IS GETTING TO BE A HABIT! MY GUN, QUICK!...

I CAN'T SHOOT—I'M AFRAID I MIGHT HIT LAURELINE!... WHERE IS THAT CREATURE TAKING HER?

THE OCEAN!

I HAVE TO RISK A SHOT... WHAT?...

THE GUMUN!... GOOD GRIEF, WHAT CARNAGE...

ARE YOU ALL RIGHT, SWEETHEART?

YES! BUT IT'S A GOOD THING THE GUMUN SHOWED UP, BECAUSE YOU...

YES! HE DID REALLY GOOD!

VALERIAN...

LAURELINE!

... I DON'T FEEL SO GOOD...

WE'RE COMING, VALERIAN!

ARGOL!!! HOW DID YOU KNOW?...

IT WAS THE GUMUN! HE LOVES YOUR FRIEND. HE SENSED THAT SHE WAS IN DANGER, AND WE MERELY HAD TO FOLLOW HIM...

... ALAS, SHE HAS FELT THE EMBRACE OF A SPLITTING SHALAFUT, AND I FEAR THAT... WAIT... WHAT IS IT YOU WISH TO DO, LOGAR?

MY DAUGHTER HAS FOUND HER GIFT!!

DEAR LOGAR! YOU SHALL BE SHE-WHO-HEALS-WOUNDS-FROM-EVIL-BEASTS! EMBRACE ME, MY DAUGHTER!

SAVED!...

YES! STILL, SOMEHOW, I'M THE ONE WHO GOT SHAFTED AGAIN! WHY NOT YOU, HUH?... EVEN SPACE CRITTERS ARE MISOGYNOUS...

FRIENDS, QUARREL NOT! RATHER COME AND SEE OUR CRAFT. WE SHALL USE IT TO HUNT THE CRUEL BUT DELECTABLE FURUTZ.

OH, BUT... YOU KNOW, I HAVE TO TAKE YOU BACK TO...

COME, NOW! MY SON SIMPLY MUST CATCH HIS FIRST FURUTZ!... STAY WITH US FOR THE GREAT HUNT!... FIRST, THOUGH, LET US CELEBRATE THE RESCUE OF YOUR FRIEND.

SOON...

NOT A BAD FEAST. A BIT HEAVY, MAYBE... NOT TO MENTION THAT WE SHOULD START THINKING ABOUT OUR MISSION...

WIMP! WE'RE NOT TIRED AT ALL, ARE WE, MY LOVELY GUMUN? ARE WE, MY BIG RESCUER?...

I'VE HAD IT UP TO HERE WITH HER GUMUN!

FRIENDS! THE SEA IS A PALE YELLOW. THIS IS GOOD FURUTZ WEATHER. AND LAGOR IS EAGER TO SEE HIS FIRST POD.

AND SOON...

WHAT WORRIES ME ARE THESE FLOATING HOUSES. I HOPE THE FURUTZ ARE STILL THERE...

THESE ARE THE PLANTS THAT EXTRACT THE SALTS FROM MAGNETOCEAN'S WATERS. WE'LL HAVE TO STAY WELL CLEAR.

SEE, LAGOR... A POD OF FURUTZ! LED BY THE STRONGEST MALE. IT IS HE WHO WILL OFFER COMBAT, AND HE YOU SHALL HAVE TO STRIKE...

FEAR NOT. THOSE THINGS HOLD NO INTEREST FOR US. HEY... LOOK... **OVER THERE!**

BUT, WHILE THE HUNT BEGINS, TO THE JOYFUL CRIES OF THE FAMILY...

SEE HOW HAPPY THEY ARE... AND HOLD YOUR COURSE! ARGOL GAVE YOU THE HELM.

I'M DOING MY BEST!!!

... BUT I'M SHORTER THAN HE IS...

AGENT VALERIAN...

OH, COME ON! BLASTED RADIO! NOW'S NOT THE TIME!!

LOOK UP, AGENT VALERIAN!

WELL, VALERIAN? HAVE YOU FORGOTTEN THAT MAGNETOCEAN IS A STRATEGIC INDUSTRIAL AREA? WARN YOUR FRIENDS...

BY SPACE! THE GOVERNOR'S AIRCRAFT—WITH A WHOLE SQUADRON! THEY'VE TRACKED US DOWN!

... THEY MUST SAIL AWAY FROM THE FLOATING EXTRACTION PLANTS OR **WE WILL OPEN FIRE!!**

33A

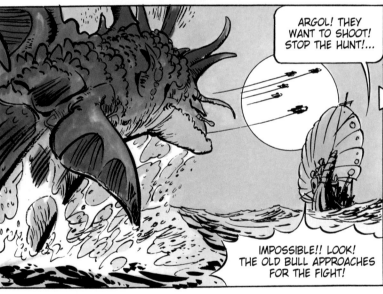

ARGOL! THEY WANT TO SHOOT! STOP THE HUNT!...

IMPOSSIBLE!! LOOK! THE OLD BULL APPROACHES FOR THE FIGHT!

AND TELL THEM THAT FURUTZ CANNOT ABIDE NOISE! A POD WITHOUT ITS LEADER IS A PANICKED POD, AND IT COULD DO TERRIBLE DAMAGE!!!

DID YOU HEAR THAT UP THERE?!

LOUD AND CLEAR! BUT THE PLANTS' PERIMETER IS STILL OFF LIMITS! VEER AWAY OR WE'LL SHOOT!

BUT... BUT... ARGOL!!!

NOW, MY SON. STEADY YOUR ARM...

YOU'VE ASKED FOR IT, VALERIAN! **FIRE**, ALL OF YOU!

32B

111

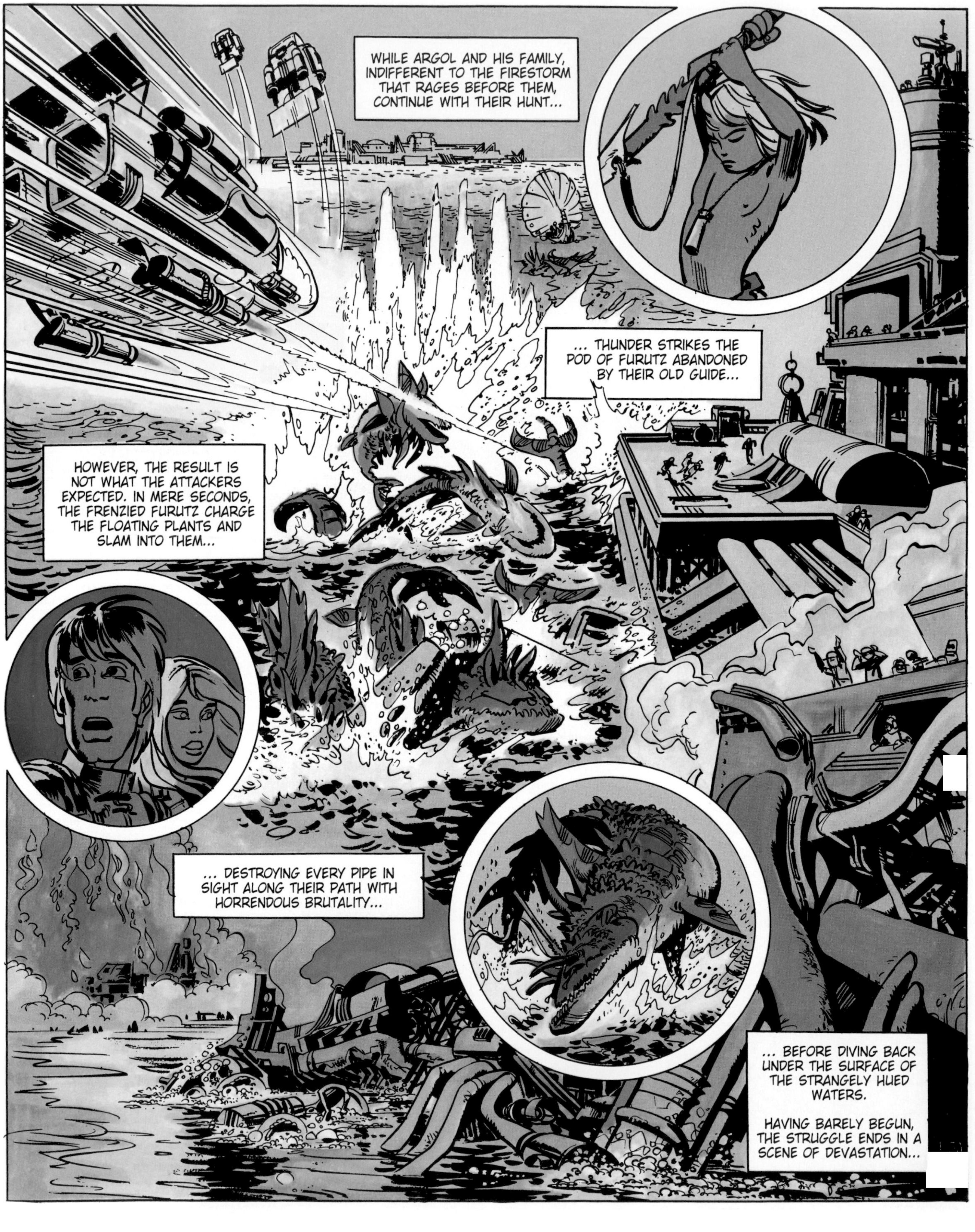
WHILE ARGOL AND HIS FAMILY, INDIFFERENT TO THE FIRESTORM THAT RAGES BEFORE THEM, CONTINUE WITH THEIR HUNT...
... THUNDER STRIKES THE POD OF FURUTZ ABANDONED BY THEIR OLD GUIDE...
HOWEVER, THE RESULT IS NOT WHAT THE ATTACKERS EXPECTED. IN MERE SECONDS, THE FRENZIED FURUTZ CHARGE THE FLOATING PLANTS AND SLAM INTO THEM...
... DESTROYING EVERY PIPE IN SIGHT ALONG THEIR PATH WITH HORRENDOUS BRUTALITY...
... BEFORE DIVING BACK UNDER THE SURFACE OF THE STRANGELY HUED WATERS.
HAVING BARELY BEGUN, THE STRUGGLE ENDS IN A SCENE OF DEVASTATION...

AT THAT MOMENT, SOMEWHERE ALONG THE SHORE OF ANANIL FOREST...

OUTSTANDING, MY SON! YOU HAVE STRUCK THE FURUTZ PRECISELY AS I TOLD YOU, IN ITS ONLY VULNERABLE SPOT! NOW YOU TRULY BELONG TO ALFLOLOL!

WHAT CARNAGE!

AGENTS OF EARTH!

IT'S THEIR FAULT-THOSE MORONS UP THERE!...

THE MORONS ARE ON THEIR WAY! STAY WHERE YOU ARE, AND WATCH THE AFLO... WHATEVER... YOUR BLASTED NOMADS!

THAT'S IT! ENOUGH PLAYING AROUND! THESE SAVAGES ARE CAUSING DISASTER AFTER DISASTER, DISORGANISING OUR PRODUCTION SYSTEM...

THAT'S NOT TRUE! IT WAS YOU WHO...

ENOUGH! IN ANY CASE, THERE'S NEWS, AND THE COUNCIL HAS MADE SOME DECISIONS!

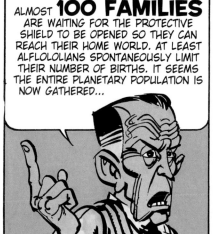

ALMOST **100 FAMILIES** ARE WAITING FOR THE PROTECTIVE SHIELD TO BE OPENED SO THEY CAN REACH THEIR HOME WORLD. AT LEAST ALFLOLOLIANS SPONTANEOUSLY LIMIT THEIR NUMBER OF BIRTHS. IT SEEMS THE ENTIRE PLANETARY POPULATION IS NOW GATHERED...

AND... THOSE DECI- SIONS?...

THE GALACTIC CODE FORBIDS US FROM BARRING THEM ACCESS TO TECHNOROG. IT ALSO FORCES US TO GIVE THEM SOME LAND BACK. VERY WELL...

FORTUNATELY, TECHNOROG IS HUGE. SO, WE'RE GOING TO REGROUP THEM IN AN AREA WE WILL DEFINE OURSELVES. THERE...

FORCE THEM ONTO A RESERVATION!
THAT'S WHAT YOU'RE GOING TO DO!!!

INDEED, A FEW HOURS LATER, AMIDST THE CHAOS AND COMMOTION OF A LONG CARAVAN FLANKED BY TERRAN SHIPS AND GUARDS...

THIS IS IT! IT'S ALL YOURS AS FAR AS YOU CAN SEE!

BUT THESE ARE THE POOREST HUNTING GROUNDS OF ALFLOLOL!!!

AND THOSE SMOKING HOUSES THERE WILL SCARE AWAY THE GAME!

NOTHING EVER PLEASES YOU NOMADS, DOES IT? NEVER MIND... IF YOU HAVE ANY COMPLAINTS, TAKE THEM TO YOUR BENEFACTOR, VALERIAN. AS FOR ME, I MUST RETURN TO TECHNOROG. INDUSTRY DOESN'T WAIT! YOU CAN UNDERSTAND THAT, HMM?...

AND, WHILE ALL TERRAN SHIPS, SAVE THOSE ASSIGNED TO WATCHING THE ALFLOLOLIAN CAMP, RETURN TO THE CITY...

I HOPE YOU'RE PROUD OF YOURSELF! TO THINK THAT YOU'RE SUPPOSED TO ADMINISTER ALL THIS...

WHAT CAN I SAY? THE ALFLOLOLIANS TRUST ME. BESIDES... I'M ONLY HERE TEMPORARILY...

THAT'S NO REASON TO GO ALONG WITH THIS TRAVESTY. ANYWAY, IT WON'T WORK...

YOU REALLY ARE A NAYSAYER! THERE'S PLENTY OF SPACE FOR EVERYONE ON ALFLOLOL, AFTER ALL!

DO YOU CALL THIS PREY, THEN, VALERIAN? LOOK AT THIS SAD, BONY PURPLINUL! THIS IS ALL WE COULD CATCH TODAY...

TASTE THIS, LITTLE ONE, AND TELL ME WHAT YOU THINK!

IT SMELLS LIKE YOUR FACTORIES THERE. DREADFUL!

AREN'T YOU HUNTING TODAY?

WE ARE IN THE SIROCCO REGION. WHEN IT BLOWS, IT DOES SO UNTIL THE END OF THE MOON! THEN, BOTH HUNTERS AND PREY HIDE.

FINALLY...

VALERIAN, THIS CAN'T GO ON!

I KNOW, I KNOW. BUT WHAT CAN I DO?

GO TO THE GOVERNOR AND TALK TO HIM! IF THE ALFLOLOLIANS MUST BE KEPT PRISONERS HERE, THEN AT LEAST THEY SHOULD BE FED!

PRISONERS... YOU'RE EXAGGERATING. STILL... YOU'RE RIGHT. I'LL CALL.

A LITTLE LATER, AT THE GOVERNOR'S PALACE...

WELL, YOU WERE BOTH VERY PERSUASIVE, OBVIOUSLY, SINCE THE COUNCIL MEMBERS WERE KIND ENOUGH TO AGREE TO YOUR SUGGESTIONS... WE'LL FEED YOUR GOOD-FOR-NOTHINGS...

THEY'RE NOT GOOD-FOR-NOTHINGS!!!

LAURELINE, PLEASE...

FOOD CONVOYS WILL LEAVE EVERY NIGHT FROM THE HYDROPONIC FARMS, BUT...

BUT BE WARNED!... THOSE BRUTES OF YOURS HAD BETTER BEHAVE. OTHERWISE...

PRODUCTION, MY CHILDREN! THE ALL-IMPORTANT PRODUCTION! WE HAVE STANDARDS TO FOLLOW, YOU UNDERSTAND? THE SLIGHTEST HICCUP, AND BANG...

AND, IN THE STILL-BLOWING SIROCCO...

THERE! THE SECOND CONVOY'S COMING...

YES... QUITE UNPALATABLE, THIS EARTH FOOD. ODOURLESS, FLAVOURLESS... AH, WELL... WE SHALL NOT STARVE...

HEAVENS! LOOK WHAT WE'VE REDUCED THE ALFLOLOLIANS TO, MY POOR GUMUN...

FOOD DISTRIBUTION! QUEUE UP...

CALL FOR YOU FROM TECHNOROROGRAD!

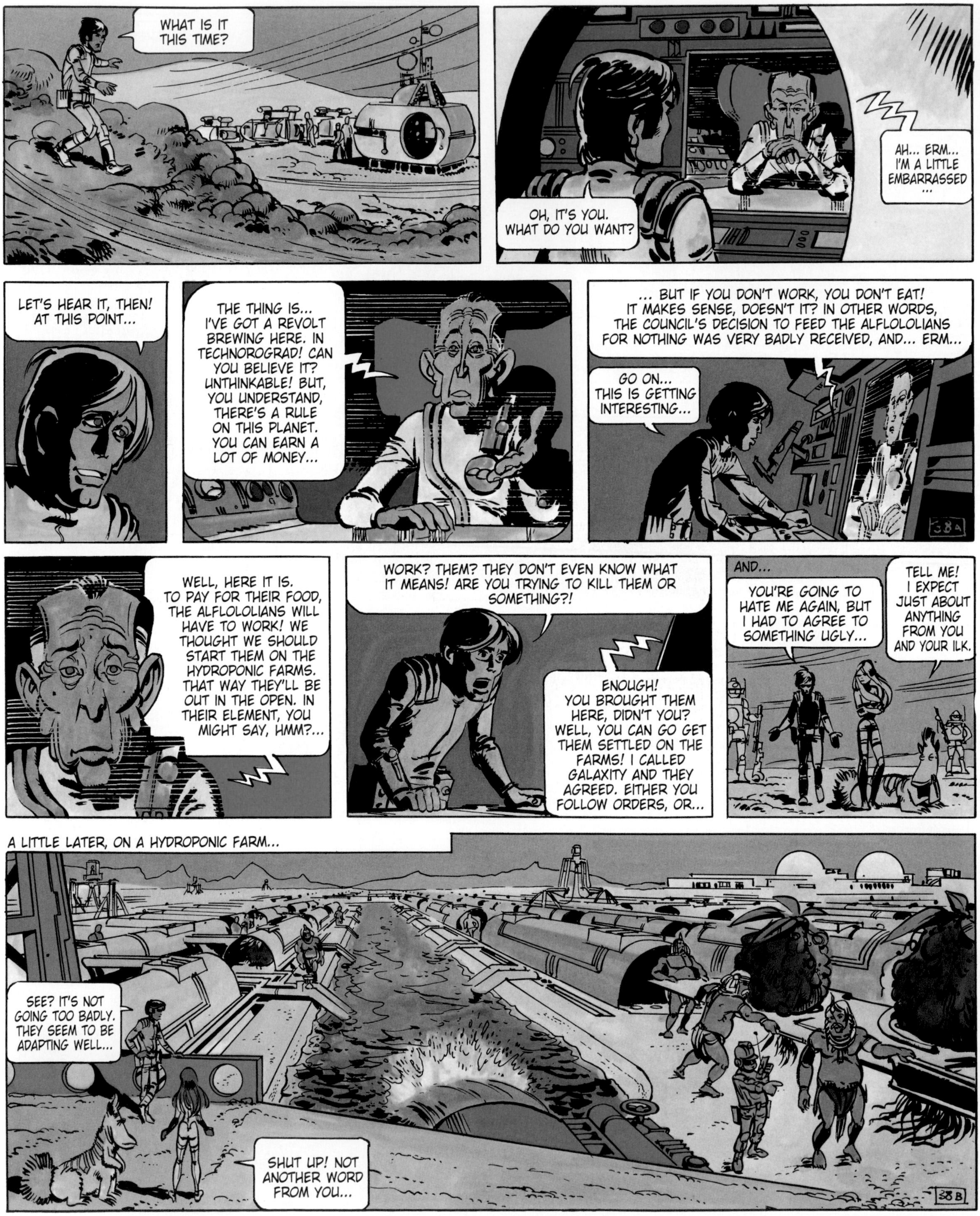
WHAT IS IT THIS TIME?
AH... ERM... I'M A LITTLE EMBARRASSED...
OH, IT'S YOU. WHAT DO YOU WANT?
LET'S HEAR IT, THEN! AT THIS POINT...
THE THING IS... I'VE GOT A REVOLT BREWING HERE. IN TECHNOROGRAD! CAN YOU BELIEVE IT? UNTHINKABLE! BUT, YOU UNDERSTAND, THERE'S A RULE ON THIS PLANET. YOU CAN EARN A LOT OF MONEY...
... BUT IF YOU DON'T WORK, YOU DON'T EAT! IT MAKES SENSE, DOESN'T IT? IN OTHER WORDS, THE COUNCIL'S DECISION TO FEED THE ALFLOLOLIANS FOR NOTHING WAS VERY BADLY RECEIVED, AND... ERM...
GO ON... THIS IS GETTING INTERESTING...
38A
WELL, HERE IT IS. TO PAY FOR THEIR FOOD, THE ALFLOLOLIANS WILL HAVE TO WORK! WE THOUGHT WE SHOULD START THEM ON THE HYDROPONIC FARMS. THAT WAY THEY'LL BE OUT IN THE OPEN. IN THEIR ELEMENT, YOU MIGHT SAY, HMM?...
WORK? THEM? THEY DON'T EVEN KNOW WHAT IT MEANS! ARE YOU TRYING TO KILL THEM OR SOMETHING?!
ENOUGH! YOU BROUGHT THEM HERE, DIDN'T YOU? WELL, YOU CAN GO GET THEM SETTLED ON THE FARMS! I CALLED GALAXITY AND THEY AGREED. EITHER YOU FOLLOW ORDERS, OR...
AND...
YOU'RE GOING TO HATE ME AGAIN, BUT I HAD TO AGREE TO SOMETHING UGLY...
TELL ME! I EXPECT JUST ABOUT ANYTHING FROM YOU AND YOUR ILK.
A LITTLE LATER, ON A HYDROPONIC FARM...
SEE? IT'S NOT GOING TOO BADLY. THEY SEEM TO BE ADAPTING WELL...
SHUT UP! NOT ANOTHER WORD FROM YOU...
38B

ACTUALLY, YOU'D BE BETTER OFF JUST LEAVING THE CAMP. WITH ALL THE GUARDS AROUND HERE, NO NEED FOR ANOTHER SPY! ANYWAY, NO ONE WANTS YOU AROUND ANYMORE... I'M STAYING HERE TO LIVE LIKE THEM...

COME, MY DARLING GUMUN. WE'RE OFF TO WORK, YOU AND I...

BUT...

BAH! LIFE SUCKS...

I'M GOING TO GO PITCH MY DOME SOMEWHERE AROUND HERE AND WAIT... WHAT ELSE CAN I DO? THE TRUTH IS, I'M NO LONGER NEEDED...

SO, SOMEWHERE IN THE MOST DESOLATE PART OF ALFLOLOL'S GREAT DESERT, WHILE THE PLANET'S LONG NIGHT STARTS TO FALL, ARTIFICIAL DAYS PASS SLOWLY INSIDE A BADLY KEPT DOME...

UNTIL...

TECHNOROGRAD CALLING VALERIAN...

YEAH!

YOU AGAIN! LEAVE ME THE HECK ALONE!!!

YOU FORGET YOURSELF, YOUNG MAN. BUT I'LL FORGIVE YOU THIS ONCE, BECAUSE YOU'RE GOING TO BE USEFUL TO ME ONE LAST TIME. I'LL MEET YOU AT THE HYDRO-PONIC FARMS ASAP. THERE'S BEEN A DISASTER. OVER.

A DISASTER? WHAT KIND OF DISASTER? BAH. LET'S GO, VALERIAN. YOU'RE PERSONA NON GRATA ANYWAY, SO...

NEAR THE FARMS...

OH! OH!

... AND ON SITE...

AH, AH! YOU ARE BACK, FRIEND! WHAT DO YOU THINK OF THIS? DOES IT NOT LOOK MORE WELCOMING ALREADY?...

ER...

AND GUESS WHO TURNED THESE NASTY PLANTS INTO LOVELY FLOWERS?... MY SON LAGOR...

FROM NOW ON, ALL SHALL KNOW HIM AS HE-WHO-HAS-THE-GIFT-TO-MAKE-UGLY-THINGS-BEAUTIFUL!

VERY GOOD, ARGOL... BUT... ER... IS ANY OF THIS EDIBLE?

EDIBLE? YOU JEST! IN ANY CASE, WHAT THE EARTHLINGS USED TO PRODUCE WAS SO BAD THAT IT MAKES LITTLE DIFFERENCE!

AGENT VALERIAN, THE GOVERNOR IS WAITING FOR YOU. HE WANTS A WORD.

COMING, COMING...

SO...

HAVE YOU SEEN WHAT THOSE BUMS DID? TECHNOROG IS ON THE VERGE OF FAMINE, AND EVEN CLOSER TO REVOLT. THE COUNCIL MET AGAIN, AND WE'VE MADE NEW DECISIONS...

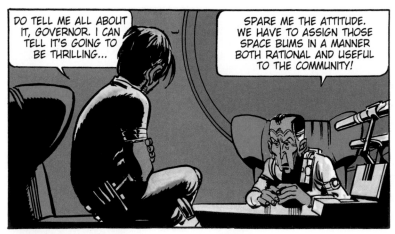

DO TELL ME ALL ABOUT IT, GOVERNOR. I CAN TELL IT'S GOING TO BE THRILLING...

SPARE ME THE ATTITUDE. WE HAVE TO ASSIGN THOSE SPACE BUMS IN A MANNER BOTH RATIONAL AND USEFUL TO THE COMMUNITY!

MAYBE IF WE SPLIT THEM UP WE CAN USE THEM MORE EFFICIENTLY. THEY ARE, AFTER ALL, STRONG AND CLEVER. THIS IS WHAT WE'VE DECIDED. ONE THIRD OF THEM WILL GO TO THE MINES, ONE THIRD TO THE FACTORIES, AND ONE THIRD TO THE POWER PLANTS...

YOU'LL BE IN CHARGE OF IMPLEMENTING THIS. AND QUICKLY.

I REFUSE...

OH, YOU REFUSE?... KNOW THIS, THEN: WHAT I HAVE HERE IS A MESSAGE FROM GALAXITY DISMISSING YOUR FRIEND LAURELINE FOR HER INEXCUSABLE BEHAVIOUR ALONGSIDE THAT INTERSTELLAR TRASH SHE SEEMS TO HAVE ADOPTED...

I CAN USE THIS MESSAGE... OR NOT. IF I USE IT, SHE'LL SPEND THE REST OF HER DAYS WORKING IN THE MINES! NO MORE SHINY SPATIO-TEMPORAL SERVICE SPACESHIPS FOR HER!

LAURE-LINE! THAT'S BLACKMAIL!!

FINE. I'LL OBEY ORDERS. THE MINES, THE FACTORIES, THE POWER PLANTS... THIS IS REALLY GOING TO BOOST PRODUCTION. I CAN FEEL IT!

KEEP YOUR SARCASM TO YOURSELF... AND REMEMBER: EVERY GUARD ON TECHNOROG IS AT YOUR DISPOSAL TO CARRY OUT YOUR ORDERS. HEADQUARTERS HAVE BEEN SET UP FOR YOU; YOU WILL STAY THERE, PLEASE. AND DO TRY TO LOOK A BIT MORE LIKE A REPRESENTATIVE OF GALAXITY...

YEAH, YEAH...

SOME TIME LATER, AS YET ANOTHER EXODUS HAS BEGUN FOR THE UNFORTUNATE ALFLOLOLIANS...

COME ON! MOVE IT, YOU DIRTY SLACKERS!

LAURELINE, SWEET LAURELINE, LET ME EXPLAIN...

DO YOU KNOW WHO THAT IS, MY GUMUN? COME ON, HURRY. WE'RE GOING TO THE FACTORIES!

BAH... WHEN IT RAINS...

YOUR AIRCRAFT FOR THE INSPECTION TOUR IS READY, AND THE GOVERNOR ASKED ME TO REMIND YOU THAT HE EXPECTS YOU IN TECHNOROGRAD WHEN YOU'RE DONE...

I KNOW. LET'S GO...

AND...

HERE ARE THE FIRST FACTORIES.

WHAT ARE THEY SUPPOSED TO BE BUILDING HERE?...

ROCKETS AND SPACESHIPS...

ARE YOU SURE ABOUT THAT? LET'S LAND.

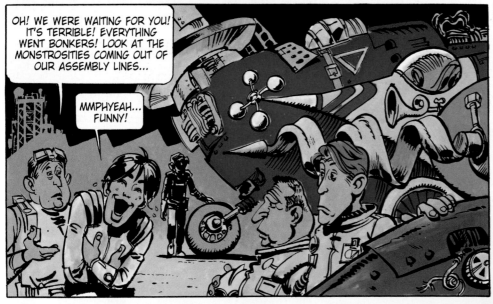

OH! WE WERE WAITING FOR YOU! IT'S TERRIBLE! EVERYTHING WENT BONKERS! LOOK AT THE MONSTROSITIES COMING OUT OF OUR ASSEMBLY LINES...

MMPHYEAH... FUNNY!

WHAT DO YOU MEAN? IT'S A TRAGEDY...

THERE'S ONE FAMILY IN PARTICULAR THAT STANDS OUT. I'M NOT SURE WHETHER THEY JUST COMPLETELY REFUSE TO COOPERATE OR THEY'RE SIMPLY RIDICULOUSLY INNOCENT...

DON'T TELL ME—I KNOW WHICH ONE! THERE'S A HUMAN WOMAN WITH THEM, ISN'T THERE?

OH, YES! LET'S TALK ABOUT THAT ONE...

WHY DON'T YOU TELL ME INSTEAD WHERE WE STAND ELSEWHERE, SINCE YOU'RE IN TOUCH WITH TECHNOROG'S OTHER INDUSTRIAL CENTRES?

IT'S A DISASTER EVERYWHERE! THE ATOMIC WEAPONS PLANT CAN'T BUILD ANYTHING BUT POCKET KNIVES...

... AND EVERYONE AT THE BIOLOGICAL CENTRE HAS A COLD...

ALL RIGHT, OFF WE GO! TO THE MINES, PAL...

YOU LOOK PRETTY CHEERFUL. HARD TO SEE WHY...

HA, HA! YOU'D BE SURPRISED! IT'S COMING TOGETHER... COME ON, STEP ON IT! MAN, THESE CRATES ARE SLOW...

AT THE MINES...

SO, HOW ARE YOUR LITTLE HOLES GOING?...

I SUPPOSE YOU MEAN OUR DRILLING? IT'S HORRIBLE. EVERYTHING'S PARALYSED HERE—LIKE EVERYWHERE ELSE...

ONCE MORE, IN THE SKIES OF TECHNOROG...

PERFECT! LET'S HAVE A QUICK LOOK AT THE POWER PLANTS AND WE CAN GO MEET THE GOVERNOR...

VERY GOOD! I DON'T THINK WE NEED TO LAND. I JUST HOPE NO ONE GOT HURT—WHICH, KNOWING THE ALFLOLOLIANS, WOULD SURPRISE ME VERY MUCH... C'MON, TO THE CITY!

FINALLY, AT THE GOVERNOR'S PALACE...

HA! LOOKS LIKE NOTHING'S WORKING!

I'M AFRAID NOT! CAN YOU IMAGINE? TODAY I HAD TO WALK HERE, ON MY FEET... FOR THE FIRST TIME IN... OH, DEAR, A LONG TIME...

FINALLY, AT THE TOP OF THE BUILDING...

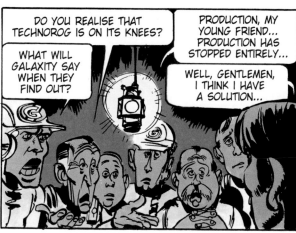

DO YOU REALISE THAT TECHNOROG IS ON ITS KNEES?

WHAT WILL GALAXY SAY WHEN THEY FIND OUT?

PRODUCTION, MY YOUNG FRIEND... PRODUCTION HAS STOPPED ENTIRELY...

WELL, GENTLEMEN, I THINK I HAVE A SOLUTION...

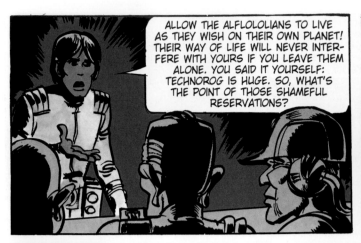

ALLOW THE ALFLOLOLIANS TO LIVE AS THEY WISH ON THEIR OWN PLANET! THEIR WAY OF LIFE WILL NEVER INTERFERE WITH YOURS IF YOU LEAVE THEM ALONE. YOU SAID IT YOURSELF: TECHNOROG IS HUGE. SO, WHAT'S THE POINT OF THOSE SHAMEFUL RESERVATIONS?

I MUST ADMIT... ERM... THAT WE'VE COME TO CONSIDER THIS SOLUTION. SINCE WE NO LONGER HAVE MUCH OF A CHOICE, WOULD YOU AGREE TO GO TELL THEM AS MUCH? THEY'LL TRUST YOU.

ER... I HOPE SO...

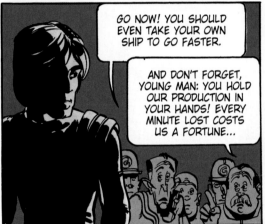

GO NOW! YOU SHOULD EVEN TAKE YOUR OWN SHIP TO GO FASTER.

AND DON'T FORGET, YOUNG MAN: YOU HOLD OUR PRODUCTION IN YOUR HANDS! EVERY MINUTE LOST COSTS US A FORTUNE...

A LITTLE LATER, IN THE STILL-DARK SKY OF ALFLOLOL-TECHNOROG...

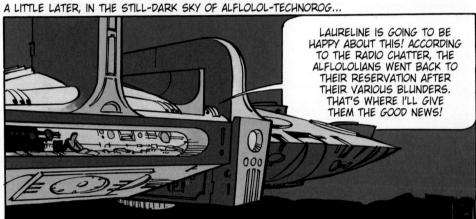

LAURELINE IS GOING TO BE HAPPY ABOUT THIS! ACCORDING TO THE RADIO CHATTER, THE ALFLOLOLIANS WENT BACK TO THEIR RESERVATION AFTER THEIR VARIOUS BLUNDERS. THAT'S WHERE I'LL GIVE THEM THE GOOD NEWS!

THERE'S THE RESERVATION. **WHAT?**...

I'LL BE!... THEY'RE ALL LEAVING!... WHAT DO I DO?...

AH, SOMEONE'S LEFT. QUICK, I'VE GOT TO LAND!!!

44B

HOW ARE YOU, FRIEND?!

OH?! LOOK WHO'S HERE.

WHY ARE THEY ALL LEAVING? I WAS COMING TO TELL THEM THEY'RE ONCE AGAIN FREE ON ALFLOLOL...

FREE ON ALFLOLOL! FREE ON A WORLD LIKE THIS! YOU REALLY HAVEN'T GOT A CLUE, MY POOR VALERIAN. THEY ALL LEFT BECAUSE THEY DON'T WANT THEIR PLANET ANYMORE. WE ONLY STAYED BECAUSE ARGOL AND HIS FAMILY HAVE LOST THEIR SHIP.

BUT... BUT...

OH, DON'T FEEL TOO BAD, MY BOY. IN YOUR OWN WAY, YOU DID ALL YOU COULD... IT JUST WASN'T THE RIGHT WAY, THAT'S ALL.

HOW ABOUT... HOW ABOUT I TAKE YOU ALL ABOARD MY SHIP? HOW ABOUT I GUIDE THE OTHERS THROUGH THE PASSES? HOW ABOUT...

AH! I EXPECTED NOTHING LESS FROM YOU!

HMM... I'VE GOT MY VALERIAN BACK!

SOON, IN THE DANGEROUSLY CROWDED VICINITY OF THE GREAT PLANET, A LONG CONVOY MOVES OFF TOWARDS OPEN SPACE...

123

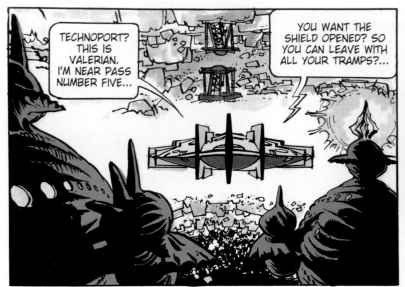

TECHNOPORT? THIS IS VALERIAN. I'M NEAR PASS NUMBER FIVE...

YOU WANT THE SHIELD OPENED? SO YOU CAN LEAVE WITH ALL YOUR TRAMPS?...

... HA! HA! THAT'S RIGHT! BUT YOU CAN BET YOUR BOTTOM CREDIT IT'S NOT ABOUT TO OPEN THE OTHER WAY AGAIN. AND THAT GOES FOR YOU BLASTED SPATIO-TEMPORAL AGENTS. TROUBLEMAKERS, SABOTEURS...

... YOU'RE LUCKY I DON'T WANT TO INFORM GALAXITY OF ALL YOUR EXPLOITS HERE; OTHERWISE...

CLICK

HE DOES GO ON, DOESN'T HE? HOW ABOUT YOU TELL ME WHAT WE'RE GOING TO DO NOW THAT WE'RE OUT? THE OTHER FAMILIES HAVE DECIDED TO GO TRAVELLING AGAIN...

I DO HAVE AN IDEA...

... A PLACE WHERE THERE ARE TASTY THINGS TO EAT AND DRINK; A PLACE WHERE WE'RE GUARANTEED A WARM WELCOME; A PLACE WHERE YOUR PARTIES WILL BE A BIG SUCCESS! WHAT DO YOU SAY, ARGOL?

ANYWHERE YOU CHOOSE, EARTHLING. WE TRUST YOU.

A LOT LATER, ON EARTH. GALAXITY SPACEPORT...

HERE THEY COME!

IS EVERYTHING READY? YOU KNOW THAT, IN ACCORDANCE WITH THE GALACTIC CODE, ALL REPRESENTATIVES OF A NEW SPECIES MUST BE WELCOMED TO EARTH WITH THE RANK OF AMBASSADORS AND OFFERED HOSPITALITY FOR AS LONG AS THEY WISH.

THE CELEBRATION WILL BE QUITE MERRY, SIR. QUITE MERRY, AND PERFECTLY ORGANISED.

THE END

SCRIPT: CHRISTIN
ARTWORK: J.C. MEZIERES

124

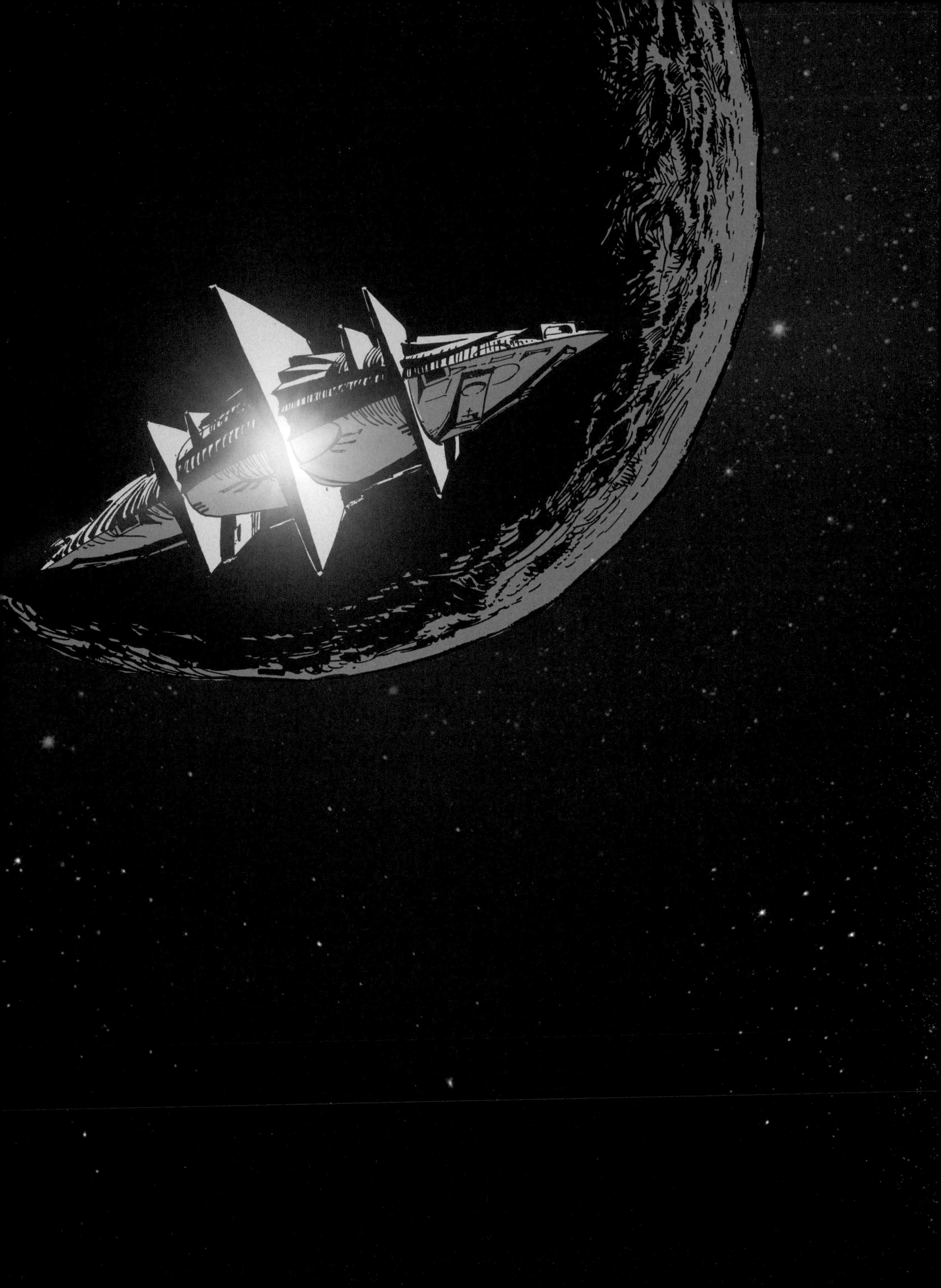

BIRDS OF THE MASTER

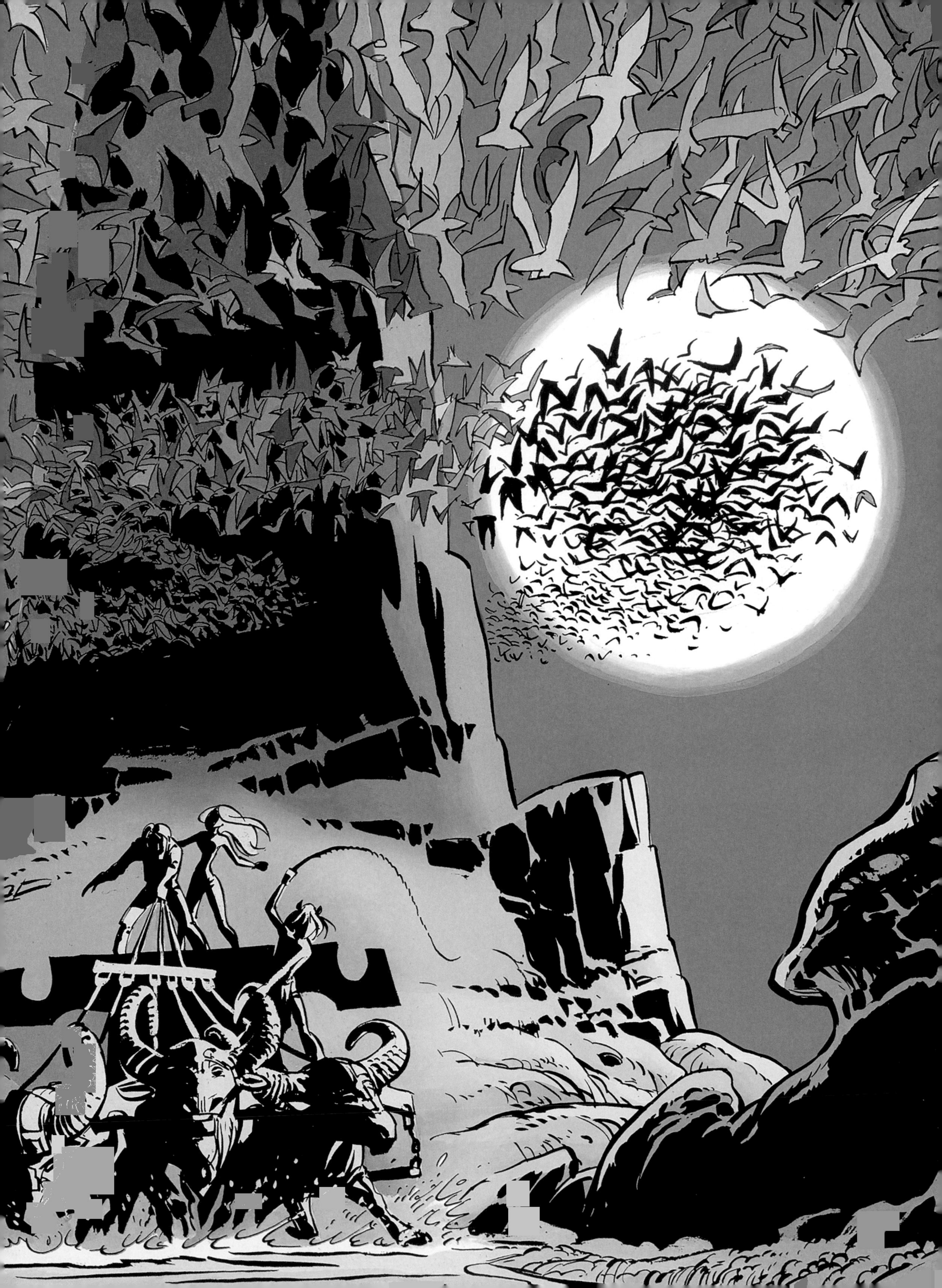

THAT WAS JUST GREAT...

WHAT WAS GREAT!?!

THAT LITTLE MECHANICAL FAILURE, FOLLOWED BY CRASHING THE SHIP IN SO MUCH MUD THE BAY DOORS ARE BLOCKED— AND THE SKIFFS WITH THEM...

A FAILURE... I'M NOT SO SURE.

THERE WAS SOMETHING ELSE... I SAW SOMETHING GO BY, LIKE... ER... LIKE A DARK CLOUD. I PASSED OUT FOR AN INSTANT, AND...

AND NOW WE'RE IN THIS CRAP!

IF YOU THINK IT'S EASY!... THIS SORRY EXCUSE FOR A RAFT ISN'T EXACTLY...

PAH!

WATCH IT!

THE CURRENTS ARE STRONG, TOO...

LOOK OVER THERE!

THIS IS WHERE MOST OF THE SHIPS DECLARED LOST IN GALAXITY MUST HAVE ENDED UP...

THERE ARE OTHERS FROM DIFFERENT SYSTEMS, TOO...

A SPACESHIP CEMETERY!

PROBABLY DRAWN HERE LIKE I WAS. THERE'S AN EVIL PRESENCE ON THIS WANDERING PLANETOID.

YEAH, MAYBE THERE'S SOMETHING TO YOUR SUDDEN BLACKOUT STORY...

AND SINCE THEY WEREN'T ON THEIR GUARD, THEY WERE HIT A LOT WORSE THAN WE WERE. ALL OF THOSE SHIPS LOOK BEYOND REPAIR...

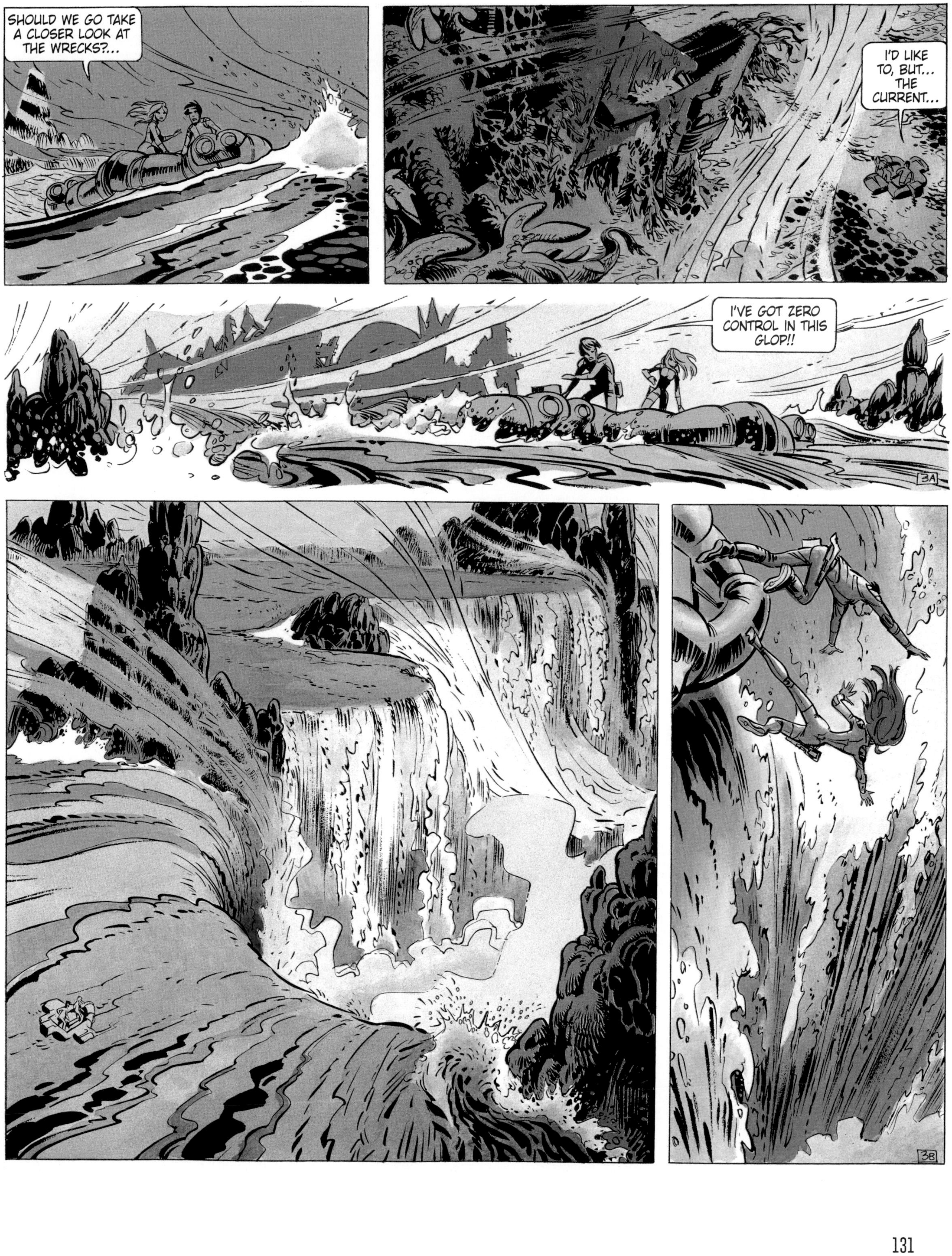
SHOULD WE GO TAKE A CLOSER LOOK AT THE WRECKS?...
I'D LIKE TO, BUT... THE CURRENT...
I'VE GOT ZERO CONTROL IN THIS GLOP!!
3A
3B

IN THE SLUGGISH CHURNING OF THE THICK FLUID...

... DRIFTING FROM EDDY TO EDDY, VALERIAN AND LAURELINE...

... ALREADY UNCONSCIOUS, COME TO REST ON A BANK OF LONG ALGAE...

SUDDENLY, PLUNGING INTO THE NOW-QUIET DEPTHS...

WELL, WAKE THEM UP!

HURRY! THE MASTER IS ALREADY MUCH DISPLEASED... OUR ALGAE HARVEST IS FAR FROM COMPLETE!...

BUT...

LOOK OUT! THEY'RE HERE!!

THE BIRDS OF MADNESS ARE COMING!!

THE MASTER MUST HAVE GUIDED YOU HERE SO YOU COULD JOIN HIS SERVICE, LIKE US! SO, GET TO WORK. QUICKLY!

WAIT... THOSE BIRDS OF MADNESS?...

LAURELINE! THAT'S WHAT I SAW WHEN I LOST CONTROL OF THE SHIP!!!

WHAT'S ALL THIS TALK OF A MASTER?... WHAT'S THAT ALL ABOUT!?...

HEY, YOU TWO!!

WE'VE FINALLY FOUND A RICH PATCH OF ALGAE. WE MUST WORK HARD TO KEEP THE MASTER'S FURY AT BAY...

ALL RIGHT, ALL RIGHT...

WHAT DO WE DO?

YOU, THE ALGAE. YOU, THE GRAPPLERS!

IN THE SILENCE OF BACKBREAKING LABOUR, THE HEAVY VESSEL RAPIDLY FILLS TO THE BRIM WITH A CARGO OF ALGAE...

... WHILE, ABOVE IT, THE BLACK, SILENT THREAT OF THE BIRDS OF MADNESS KEEPS CIRCLING...

HEY, YOU'RE HUMAN... TELL ME...

SHHH! BE SILENT... THE MASTER'S BIRDS... WORK!

?!

AT LAST...

THAT'S ENOUGH! WE'RE GOING BACK TO THE VILLAGE. EVERYONE TO THE WHEELS; WE MUST MAKE UP LOST TIME.

THE BIRDS OF MADNESS ARE LEAVING. THE MASTER IS SATISFIED WITH US...

AS THE SHIP SAILS AWAY FROM THE CENTRE OF THE LAKE...

VALERIAN! WHAT'S GOING ON? THEY ALL LOOK SO TERRIFIED!

I DON'T UNDERSTAND. OUR PRESENCE DOESN'T SEEM TO SURPRISE THEM, THOUGH...

PFFF... IF YOU WANT MY OPINION, THESE GUYS ARE ALL CRAZY!... WORK FOR THE MASTER AND HIS POULTRY—THAT'S ALL THEY KNOW...

HARVEST ALGAE AND LOTS OF TASTY FOODSTUFFS, WHILE WE EAT ROOTS AND STARVE...

... ALL THAT TO FEED THE MASTER... YOU'VE GOTTA BE NUTS, RIGHT?

LIFE HERE DOESN'T SEEM EASY...

JUST WAIT UNTIL WE'RE BACK AT THE VILLAGE. YOU'LL SEE—EVEN THE KIDS ARE STARVING. SO MUCH WORK FOR THAT BASTARD M...

HEY, YOU!...

YOU KNOW WHAT'S GOING TO HAPPEN TO YOU! MAYBE IT WAS YOU THE BIRDS OF MADNESS WERE LOOKING FOR EARLIER...

BAH! IF I...

SILENCE!

IT'S A MIRACLE THE MASTER'S WRATH HASN'T STRUCK YOUR REBELLIOUS HIDE—AND US WITH IT!!!

THERE'S THE VILLAGE! THE OTHERS ARE BACK ALREADY!

WHAT HARVEST?

WE WERE LUCKY! WE FOUND A RICH SPOT WHILE RESCUING THESE TWO. IF NOT FOR THAT...

GOOD. WE'RE ALMOST DONE HERE. WE CAN GET UNDERWAY SOON...

HEY, YOU, DOWN BELOW! CHANGE YOUR CLOTHES BEFORE WE LEAVE. HERE ARE SOME WORK FROCKS! WE MUST BE HUMBLE TO SERVE THE MASTER.

URK! THESE RAGS ARE DISGUSTING!

WORK! WORK! IS THAT THE ONLY WORD THEY KNOW!?

YEP! AND SEE THE RESULT? WE LIVE LIKE ANIMALS... WHEN I THINK ABOUT MY BEAUTIFUL PLANET...

WHERE ARE YOU FROM, KID?

MANADIL, IN THE CYGNUS CONSTELLATION. MY NAME'S SÜL.

MY ACADEMY'S TRAINING SHIP CRASHED HERE NOT TOO LONG AGO. I DON'T PLAN ON ROTTING HERE, THOUGH, LET ME TELL YOU...

WHAT DO YOU MEAN?

MEH... YOU'LL SEE! YOU TWO DON'T SEEM TO BE LIKE THE OTHERS. PIECE OF ADVICE, THOUGH... I SAW YOUR WEAPONS! KEEP THEM WELL HIDDEN, OR ELSE...

PFFF... SOME MISSIONS ARE ALL ABOUT CHIC, BUT THIS TIME...

SOON, WITH THE LAST PREPARATIONS OVER...

... THE FLOTILLA GETS UNDERWAY...

137

SLOWLY TRAVELLING THROUGH A LAND... ... WHERE SLIMY SWAMPS MAKE WAY... ... FOR A MAZE OF STEEP-SIDED FJORDS...

... AFTER MANY LONG HOURS, THE SHIPS REACH A BARREN COVE.

AND...

FORM THE CARAVAN! **GET MOVING!!**

HURRY, HURRY... THE MASTER IS WAITING...

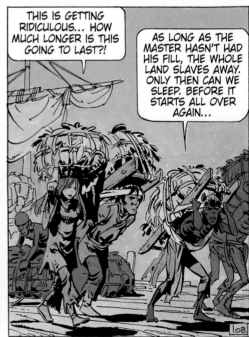

THIS IS GETTING RIDICULOUS... HOW MUCH LONGER IS THIS GOING TO LAST?!

AS LONG AS THE MASTER HASN'T HAD HIS FILL, THE WHOLE LAND SLAVES AWAY. ONLY THEN CAN WE SLEEP. BEFORE IT STARTS ALL OVER AGAIN...

ME? OH, YEAH, I AM... BUT I'M HUNGRY, YOU SEE. BESIDES, ON MANADIL WE'RE FREE. SO, LIVING LIKE THIS AIN'T LIVING.

TELL ME, SÜL: THE WAY YOU TALK ABOUT THE MASTER... AREN'T YOU AFRAID OF HIM?

LOOK, THERE'S THE VILLAGE OF FRUITS!

HEY, THERE ARE BIRDS OF MADNESS ABOVE IT!

A NEW CARAVAN, LOADED WITH SCRUMPTIOUS FRUITS, JOINS THE PEOPLE FROM THE LAKE VILLAGE.

YEAH... SOMETHING MUST HAVE HAPPENED AND THE MASTER STRUCK.

LAZINESS... CRWEAK... IS THE DAUGHTER OF WISDOM.

WHAT DID I TELL YOU! ANOTHER ONE THE MASTER DROVE INSANE!

ARE YOU EVER GOING TO EXPLAIN TO US WHO THIS MASTER IS?

THE MASTER!?! HA HA! HA!

COME ON, NOW! NO ONE KNOWS WHO THE MASTER IS! THE ONLY CERTAINTY IS THAT HE CALLS THOSE HE CHOOSES TO HIS SERVICE... AND THAT YOU HAVE TO OBEY HIM....

SOME OF US WERE BORN HERE. OTHERS ARRIVED SO LONG AGO THAT THEY'VE FORGOTTEN ABOUT THEIR PAST LIFE...

YOU KNOW, ON THE MASTER'S LANDS, YOU WALK OR YOU DIE...

WAIT... THAT WOMAN IS EXHAUSTED... WE HAVE TO DO SOMETHING.

WHAT ABOUT HER?

CLOSE RANKS! YOU, THERE, PICK UP THAT WOMAN'S LOAD!

DO AS YOU'RE TOLD! THE MASTER'S LAW PUNISHES THE REBELLIOUS AND THE LAZY!   LOOK...

ADVANCING THROUGH A TALL, DAMP-SMELLING FOREST, THE CARAVAN WALKS ON, LEAVING THE CRIPPLED BEHIND...

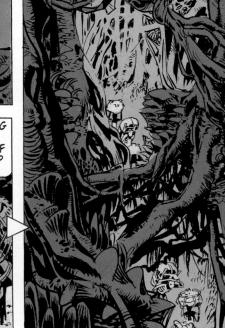

OH... I MAY BE... SCRITCH... LAZY, BUT I'M ALIVE... CLICK... CAP'N!

LEAVE IT... NOTHING WE CAN DO FOR HER. SHE'LL DIE OF EXHAUSTION. HELP ME INSTEAD...

... JOINED, AS IT PASSES VAST PLAINS, BY THE ENVOYS OF NEW VILLAGES, HERDING FAT ANIMALS BEFORE THEM...

... AND FURTHER ON BY THE CARRIERS OF MYSTERIOUS DRINKS, THEIR MOUTHWATERING SMELLS WAFTING.

AT LAST, AFTER MANY EXHAUSTING HOURS OF WALKING...

... IT ARRIVES AT AN IMMENSE VALLEY COVERED BY STORM CLOUDS AND REGULARLY SHAKEN BY BLASTS OF THUNDER.

SO, THIS IS WHERE THE CITIES OF THE MASTER LIE!

YES! AND THEY SAY IT'S AT THE VERY END, WHERE THE MISTS NEVER LIFT, THAT THE MASTER LIVES...

BUT NO ONE'S EVER GONE TO SEE, HUH?...

SOON THEY ENTER THE FOUL-SMELLING
OUTSKIRTS OF THE CITY THE CARAVAN HAS
COME TO RESUPPLY.

ALONG NARROW STREETS WHERE
CRAFTSMEN WORK TIRELESSLY IN
THE SERVICE OF THE MASTER...

... THROUGH DISTRICTS WHERE
ARTISTS ARE DECORATING THE
STONE WALLS...

... THE NEWCOMERS FINALLY REACH THE
CENTRE OF THE CITY.

142

ALL THIS TO PREPARE THE MASTER'S FOOD?

SO, WHAT DO YOU THINK, HUH? WORK, WORK, WORK... THIS IS WHERE THE COOKING MAGIC HAPPENS...

OF COURSE! BELIEVE ME, IT'S NO PICNIC TO ACHIEVE THE FINAL RESULT!

GREAT! YOU AND YOUR BLASTED HANDS-ON EXPLORATION... I'M BEAT!

OH! WE'RE STILL NOT DONE?...

QUICK! THE BIRDS OF MADNESS ARE HERE! GET TO WORK!

HERE WE GO AGAIN! THAT GUY'S LIKE A BROKEN RECORD!

WHILE VALERIAN, NAUSEATED BY THE CLOYING SMELL OF BLOOD, IS SENT TO A SLAUGHTERHOUSE TEAM...

... LAURELINE AND SÜL ARE KEPT BUSY WITH THE CRUSHERS THAT PROCESS THE FRUITS AND ALGAE.

YOU GOING TO FAINT, YOU SISSY? JUST START CUTTING UP THAT SMOOGLOF, AND HURRY UP...

COME ON! COME ON! THE GREAT MEAL IS NEVER LATE!

AT LAST, AMIDST THE LAST-MINUTE BUSTLE...

LET THE MASTER BE SERVED! OPEN THE GATES!!!

COME WITH ME! IT'S THE CEREMONY OF THE KLAAR. YOU'VE GOT TO SEE THIS!

... VATS FULL OF SCALDING JUICES, TRANSLUCENT CUPS FILLED TO THE BRIM WITH STRANGE, MULTI-COLOURED DRINKS...

WITH SPECTACULAR POMP, WHERE EVERY GESTURE SEEMS TO HAVE BEEN ARRANGED FOR ALL ETERNITY...

... AROMATIC MEATS, WONDERFULLY DRESSED AND ACCOMPANIED BY DISHES OF SPICES AND FLAGONS OF SAUCE...

... ALTOGETHER, A PRODIGIOUS FEAST MAKES ITS WAY TO THE GREAT BASIN, WATCHED BY THE STARVING CROWD SLOWLY GATHERING AROUND THE SHRINE.

IT'S DISGUSTING, ALL THIS CHOW PASSING US BY! TO THINK THAT ALL WE'LL GET AFTERWARDS IS A SHOT AT THE LEFTOVERS...

AND, TO TOP IT OFF, THE BIRDS ARE HERE TO MAKE SURE EVERYTHING GOES SMOOTHLY. DAMNED CRITTERS! I'LL KILL 'EM!

SÜL!

MASTER! THE KLAAR IS READY!

YOUR SATISFACTION MAKES YOUR PEOPLE HAPPY!

POUR!

SUDDENLY, AS THE GLOWING, AROMATIC KLAAR BEGINS TO FLOW...

DOING THAT IN FRONT OF SO MANY STARVING PEOPLE... IT'S JUST WRONG!

SURE IS... ALL THE BETTER TO MAKE US REMEMBER OUR PLACE...

... A MAN PEELS OFF FROM THE CROWD AND RUSHES TOWARDS THE BASIN...

... BUT BEFORE HE EVEN REACHES THE TEMPTING, FORBIDDEN MEAL, THE MASTER'S TERRIBLE WINGED MESSENGERS ARE UPON HIM...

THE BIRDS OF MADNESS!

AND ANOTHER ONE DRIVEN INSANE! ENOUGH OF THAT!

SÜL! NO!

145

BACK, YOU MONSTERS! I'M NOT AFRAID OF YOUR MASTER! I'M NOT!!!

NOT AFRAID!

THE BIRDS... WHY SO MEAN?...

NOT AFRAID! AAAAH!

LITTLE SÜL! IT'S HORRIBLE!!!

LEAVE IT! YOU CAN'T HELP!

CHILDREN APPROACH NOW, CARRYING BASKETS FILLED WITH THE MEAGRE LEFTOVERS OF THE MASTER'S FEAST, AND...

147

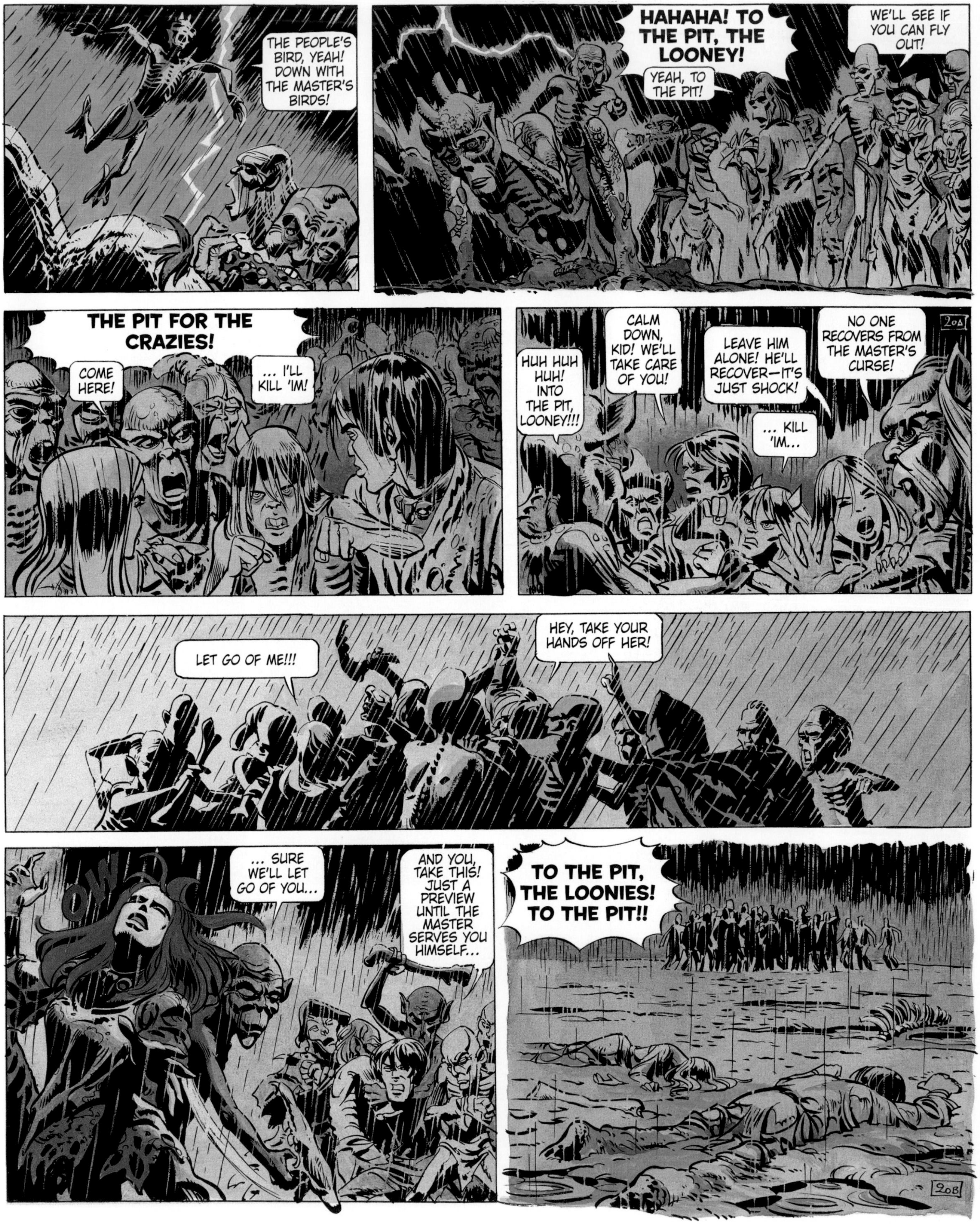
THE PEOPLE'S BIRD, YEAH! DOWN WITH THE MASTER'S BIRDS!
HAHAHA! TO THE PIT, THE LOONEY!
YEAH, TO THE PIT!
WE'LL SEE IF YOU CAN FLY OUT!
THE PIT FOR THE CRAZIES!
COME HERE!
... I'LL KILL 'IM!
HUH HUH HUH! INTO THE PIT, LOONEY!!!
CALM DOWN, KID! WE'LL TAKE CARE OF YOU!
LEAVE HIM ALONE! HE'LL RECOVER—IT'S JUST SHOCK!
NO ONE RECOVERS FROM THE MASTER'S CURSE!
... KILL 'IM...
20A
LET GO OF ME!!!
HEY, TAKE YOUR HANDS OFF HER!
OW
... SURE WE'LL LET GO OF YOU...
AND YOU, TAKE THIS! JUST A PREVIEW UNTIL THE MASTER SERVES YOU HIMSELF...
TO THE PIT, THE LOONIES! TO THE PIT!!
20B

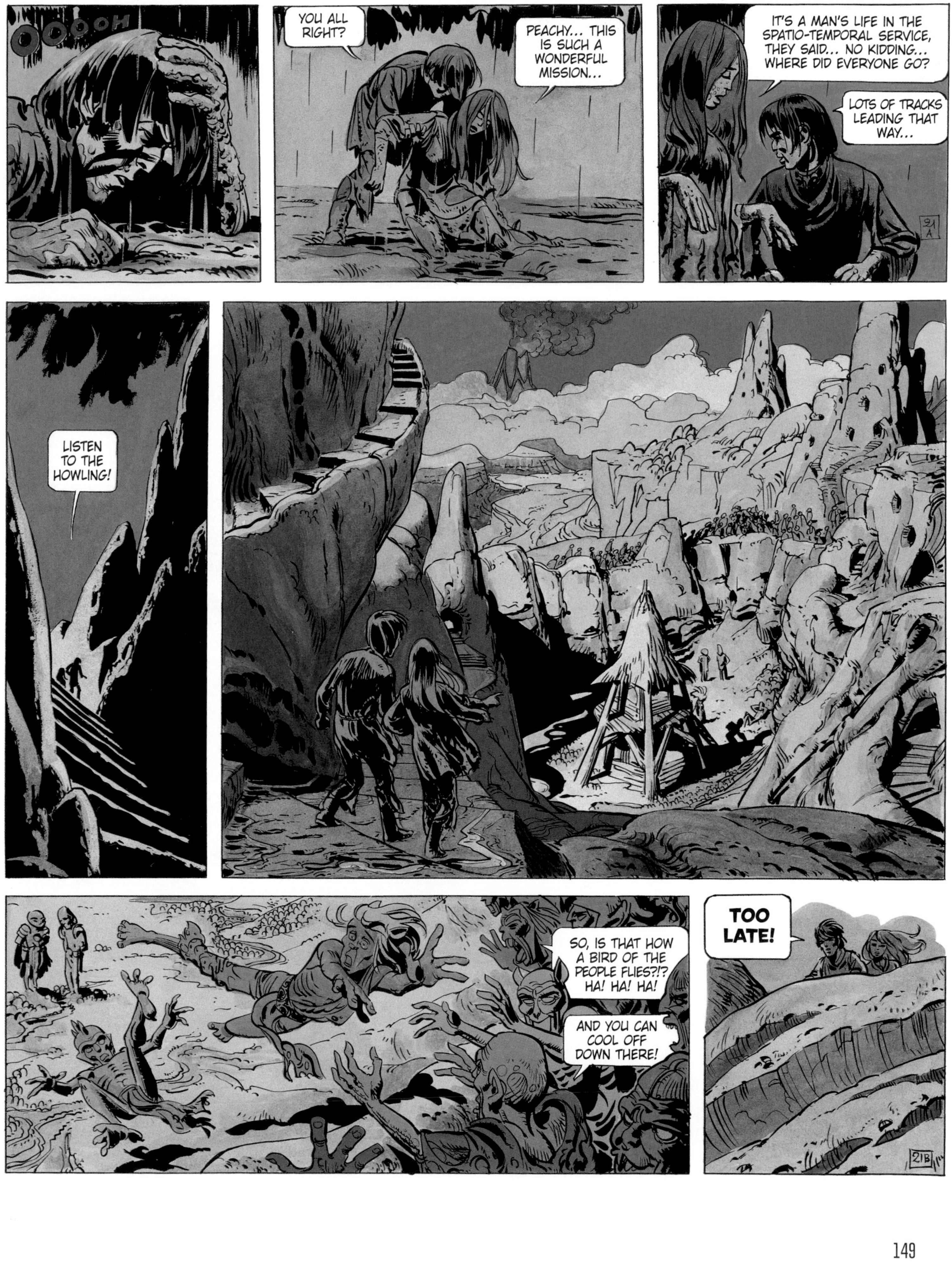
OOOOH
YOU ALL RIGHT?
PEACHY... THIS IS SUCH A WONDERFUL MISSION...
IT'S A MAN'S LIFE IN THE SPATIO-TEMPORAL SERVICE, THEY SAID... NO KIDDING... WHERE DID EVERYONE GO?
LOTS OF TRACKS LEADING THAT WAY...
LISTEN TO THE HOWLING!
SO, IS THAT HOW A BIRD OF THE PEOPLE FLIES?!? HA! HA! HA!
AND YOU CAN COOL OFF DOWN THERE!
TOO LATE!

WHERE WAS I? OH, YES... I MAINTAIN THAT THE MASTER ONLY EXISTS BECAUSE... EURG... WE ADMIT HIS EXISTENCE. OTHERWISE...

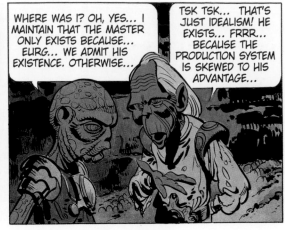

TSK TSK... THAT'S JUST IDEALISM! HE EXISTS... FRRR... BECAUSE THE PRODUCTION SYSTEM IS SKEWED TO HIS ADVANTAGE...

HEY, THEY DON'T SOUND THAT CRAZY TO ME!

... IT'S ACTUALLY THE FIRST INTELLIGENT THING I'VE HEARD IN A LONG TIME!

I IMAGINE YOU... SHHH... WERE ALSO ON A SURPRISE SPACE CRUISE, YOUNG MAN?

THEN... SCRITCH... YOU WON'T MIND SIGNING OUR PETITION? WE'LL SEND IT TO THAT MASTER OF THEIRS. WE WANT TO PROTEST THE TERRIBLE ORGANISATION AND WELCOME. WE'RE ALL FOR SURPRISES... EURG... BUT STILL...

WHY ARE YOU WORKING SO DARNED HARD?... PSHWICK... THE SEARCH FOR HAPPINESS REQUIRES PRESERVING ONE'S ENERGETIC POTENTIAL, BELIEVE ME...

BACK ON ALDEBARAN, I'M A PROSPECTOR, FIRST CLASS. SO... BLOOK... I'M PROSPECTING. I DON'T GIVE A FIG ABOUT THE MASTER.

I DON'T KNOW IF THEY'RE REALLY CRAZY, BUT...

... WE CAN'T LET THEM ROT DOWN THERE...

HEY, IT'S...

VALERIAN! LAURELINE!!

GET ME OUT OF HERE, OR I'LL HAVE TO GO WHACK THE MASTER ON MY OWN!!

YIKES... THAT WAS RASH...

LISTEN TO ME, ALL OF YOU! PLEASE...

IT'S THOSE TWO AGAIN!...

WHY IS THE MASTER SPARING THEM?

THEY'VE JUST ARRIVED! IT WAS OUR CREW WHO RESCUED THEM.

TRY TALKING TO THEM. SOMETIMES IT WORKS...

... WHY LEAVE THOSE POOR SOULS IN THAT PIT? WHY REJECT THEM WHEN THEY'RE SONS AND DAUGHTERS OF SPACE LIKE YOU? WHY BE AFRAID OF THE VILLAINOUS MASTER WHO STARVES YOU? WHEN, ALL TOGETHER, UNITED IN COMMON ENDEAVOUR, YOU COULD RESTORE YOUR DIGNITY AND RECOVER YOUR FREEDOM!... WHEN PEACE AND LOVE COULD FLOURISH ON THIS WORLD WHOSE RICHES ONLY AWAIT...

MAN, HE SUCKS TODAY...

TO THE PIT!

LET'S TEACH THEM A LESSON!

I DON'T THINK YOU REACHED THEM...

BOOH BOOH

WHAT WOULD THE MASTER BECOME WITHOUT US?

BOOH

THEY'RE LOONIER THAN THE LOONIES! WHY CHANGE ANYTHING?

GET BACK OR I SHOOT!

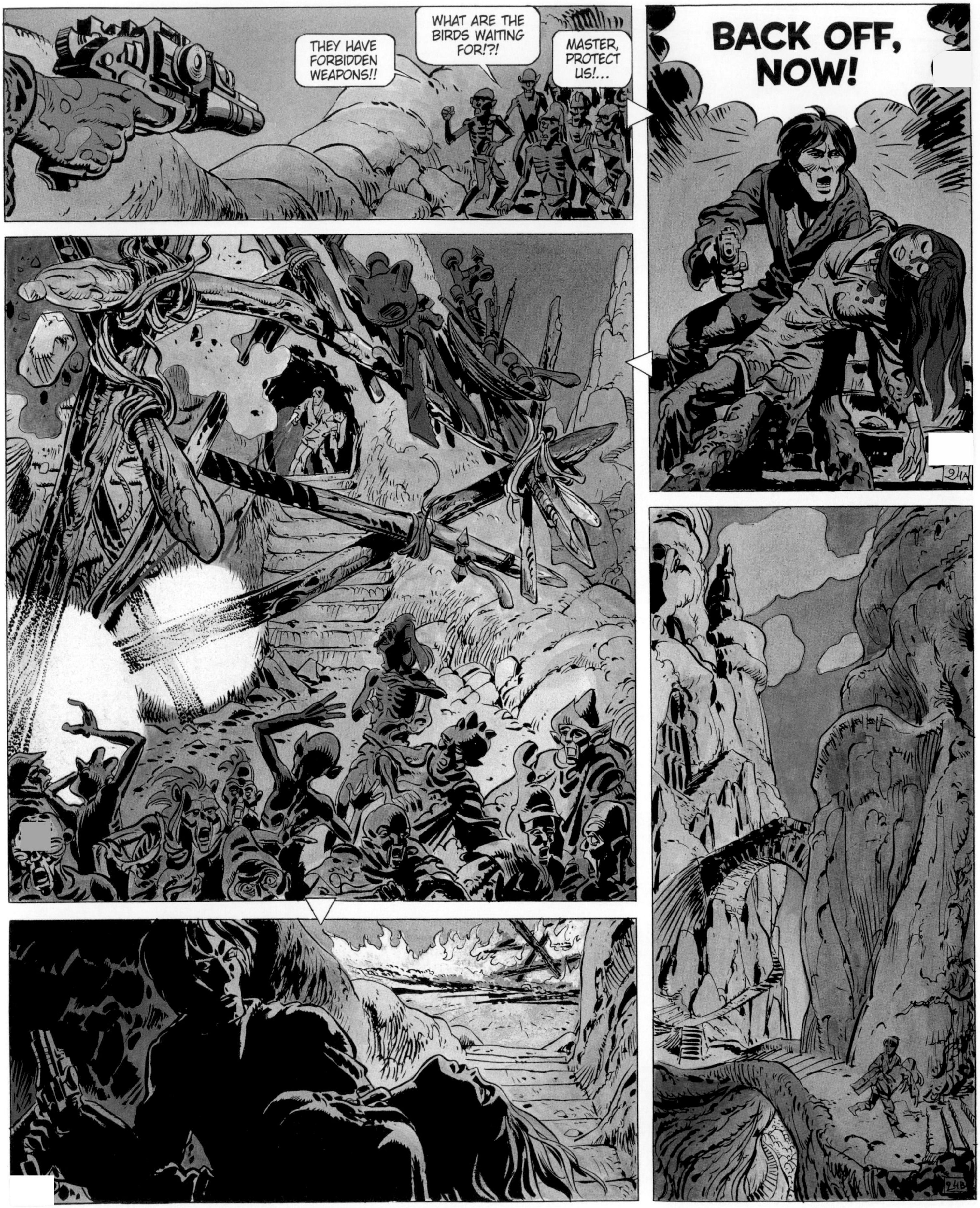
THEY HAVE FORBIDDEN WEAPONS!!
WHAT ARE THE BIRDS WAITING FOR!?!
MASTER, PROTECT US!...
BACK OFF, NOW!
24A
24B

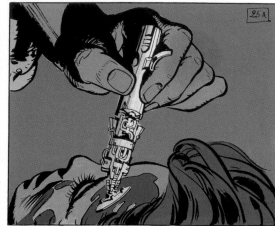

BETTER AND BETTER, BUDDY...

I'VE ALREADY BEEN DROWNED, DRESSED LIKE A HAG, FORCED TO WORK LIKE A SLAVE, KNOCKED OUT AND NOW STONED...

HOW ARE YOU FEELING?

... SO, IF YOU MUST KNOW, I'VE HAD ENOUGH! ENOUGH! ENOUGH!!! IF THEY LOVE WORKING FOR THEIR MASTER SO MUCH, LET THEM! I WANT TO GO BACK TO THE SHIP!...

SO THERE!

ERM... WHAT ABOUT SÜL? DO YOU REALLY THINK WE CAN ABANDON HIM?

LOOK! THEY'RE READY TO GO TO SLEEP... TONIGHT THEY CAN REST, BEFORE THE CARAVANS RETURN TO THE MASTER'S RESOURCE-PRODUCING VILLAGES...

HOW ABOUT WE TRY AND GET THE KID OUT ONCE THEY'RE ASLEEP, HMM? AFTER THAT, I PROMISE, WE CAN GO...

A LITTLE LATER...

ALL RIGHT, EVERY-ONE'S OUT...

SO ARE THEY, DON'T YOU THINK?

JUST AS WELL...

... BECAUSE...

... I'D RATHER WE...

... DIDN'T MAKE TOO MUCH NOISE...

PLOTCH

BRAOUM

SPLAT

YOU! HEY, I... CRWEAK... KNEW THAT I COULD COUNT ON YOU TO GO... CLACK... WHACK THE MASTER. AIN'T IT SO?

AIN'T IT? AIN'T IT? I AIN'T AFRAID, YOU KNOW... CRITCH... WE'RE ALL GOING TO ATTACK HIM...

OF COURSE WE'RE GOING, SÜL, LITTLE BUDDY, BUT FIRST...

ATTACK THE MASTER? IF YOU'RE COUNTING ON US...

... YOU'D BETTER... PLICK... HURRY THINGS UP, YOUNG MAN. BECAUSE...

HOLD ON...

HEY! I'M NOT LIKING THIS CONVERSATION. THIS ISN'T EXACTLY WHAT WE DISCUSSED...

WE'RE NOT GOING TO... CRRR... BE CRAZY MUCH LONGER. WE'RE NEW HERE, BUT... URRK... THE VENOM THOSE BLASTED BIRDS INJECTED US WITH WHEN THEY BIT US WILL SOON TAKE EFFECT...

I DISAGREE... SBRUCK... I DON'T THINK IT'S A VENOM, BUT, RATHER, THE IDEA OF THEM WE HAVE...

I SAY!... BRRR... I RECOGNISE YOU! YOU WERE ONE OF THE ORGANISERS OF OUR SURPRISE CRUISE...

I CERTAINLY HOPE... BLUCK... THAT YOU'RE GOING TO TAKE US TO SEE THAT MASTER CHARACTER AND THAT... PLOOTCH... THE STANDARD OF ACCOMMODATION WILL IMPROVE...

WE'LL DISCUSS IT LATER...

COME NOW, MY FRIEND!... BINK... ALL THOSE POOR SERVANTS OF THE MASTER YOU SAW UP THERE WERE BITTEN IN THEIR TIME. THAT IS WHY THEY ARE SO DOCILE.

NONSENSE... SCRITCH... YOU KNOW FULL WELL THAT MOST OF THEM OBEY... PLOCK... OUT OF SHEER CONFORMITY!

WAHHHH... WHAT'S GOING ON? I... BRRRRR... WAS SLEEPING!

WHAT'S ALL THIS HULLABALOO? OBEYING... PLUTCH... THE MASTER OR OBEYING SOMEONE ELSE... WHAT MATTERS IS PROSPECTING.

YOU WERE MUCH MORE ELEGANT... BLLBLL... THE LAST TIME I SAW YOU IN THE OFFICES OF...

A REFUND!... CRACK... THAT'S WHAT IT'LL COST YOU IF OUR PETITION ISN'T ACCEPTED!

WHAT I WANT IS PROPER TERRAIN, SEE, NOT LIKE... SCRITCH... THIS MUDHOLE HERE...

ERM... I DON'T WANT TO RUSH ANYONE, BUT...

WHAT'S CERTAIN... PROTCH... IS THAT THE BIRDS OF MADNESS ARE GOING TO MAKE US LIKE THE OTHER WORKERS...

NOT AT ALL!... PLOP... NO ONE IS LIKE ANYONE ELSE ON THIS PLANETOID.

DUDES ARE GONNA DAMAGE THEIR BRAINS... SPLURRR... THINKING SO MUCH! IT AIN'T GOOD SO SOON AFTER WAKING UP...

AGAINST THE MASTER... SHHHHH... THE PEOPLE'S BIRD WILL TAKE FLIGHT!!

... THE ESCAPE'S THIS WAY!

ESCAPE? WHAT ESCAPE?

THAT'S TRUE, ACTUALLY. MAYBE WE COULD STAY HERE. HERE IS FUN. WE'RE LEARNING A LOT OF AMUSING THINGS HERE...

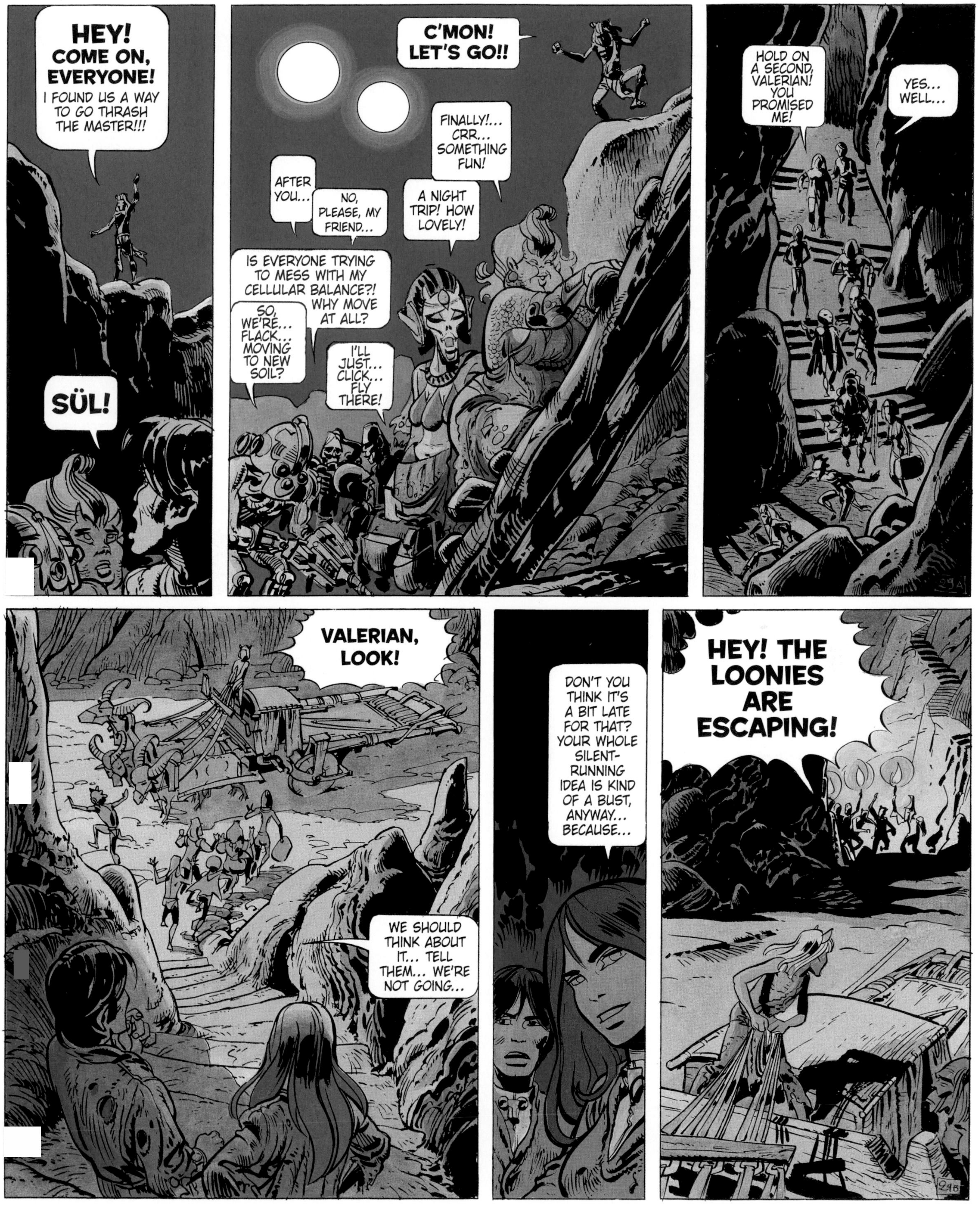
HEY! COME ON, EVERYONE! I FOUND US A WAY TO GO THRASH THE MASTER!!!
SÜL!
C'MON! LET'S GO!!
FINALLY!... CRR... SOMETHING FUN!
AFTER YOU...
NO, PLEASE, MY FRIEND...
A NIGHT TRIP! HOW LOVELY!
IS EVERYONE TRYING TO MESS WITH MY CELLULAR BALANCE?! WHY MOVE AT ALL?
SO, WE'RE... FLACK... MOVING TO NEW SOIL?
I'LL JUST... CLICK... FLY THERE!
HOLD ON A SECOND, VALERIAN! YOU PROMISED ME!
YES... WELL...
VALERIAN, LOOK!
WE SHOULD THINK ABOUT IT... TELL THEM... WE'RE NOT GOING...
DON'T YOU THINK IT'S A BIT LATE FOR THAT? YOUR WHOLE SILENT-RUNNING IDEA IS KIND OF A BUST, ANYWAY... BECAUSE...
HEY! THE LOONIES ARE ESCAPING!

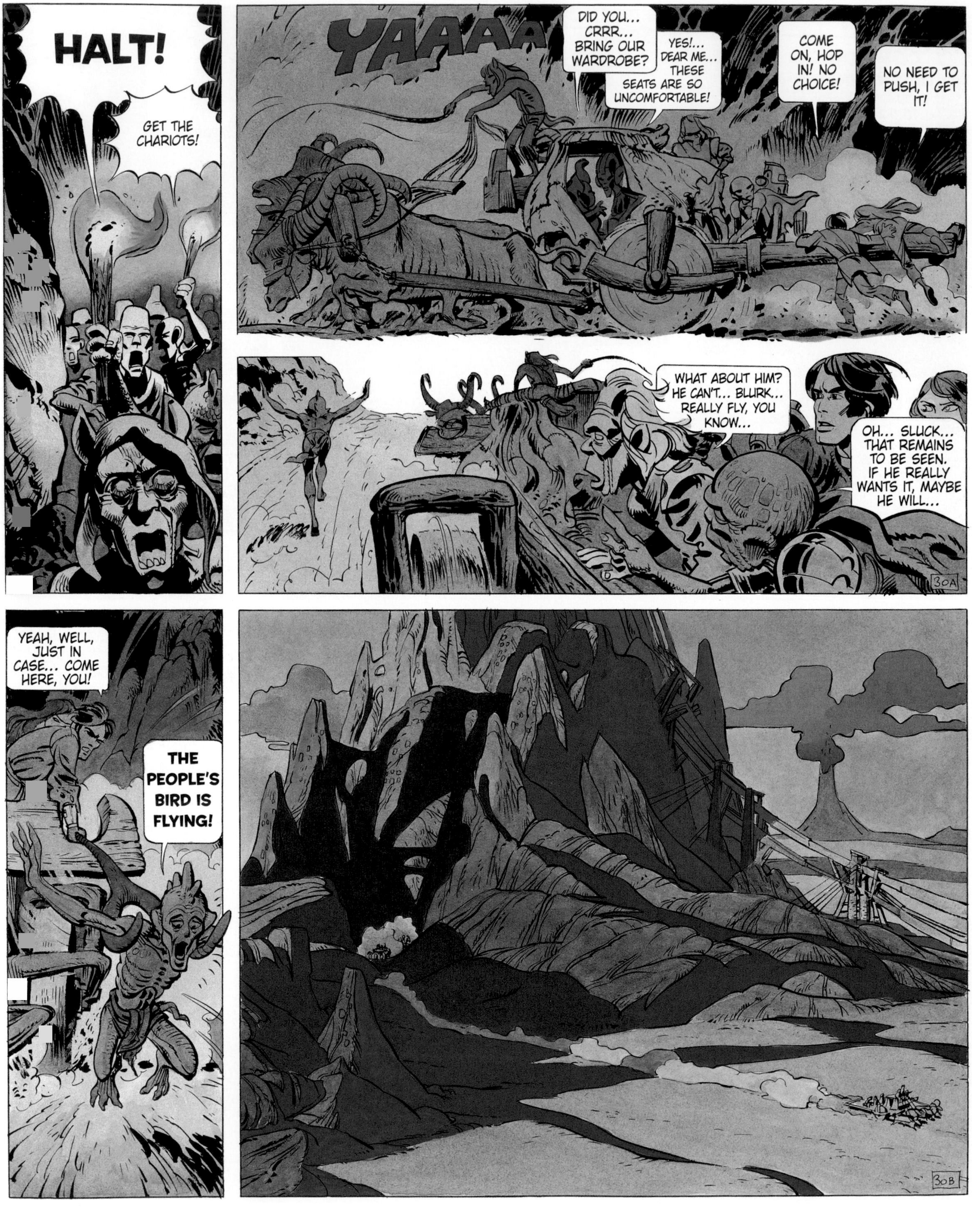

HALT!
GET THE CHARIOTS!
YAAAA
DID YOU... CRRR... BRING OUR WARDROBE?
YES!... DEAR ME... THESE SEATS ARE SO UNCOMFORTABLE!
COME ON, HOP IN! NO CHOICE!
NO NEED TO PUSH, I GET IT!
WHAT ABOUT HIM? HE CAN'T... BLURK... REALLY FLY, YOU KNOW...
OH... SLUCK... THAT REMAINS TO BE SEEN. IF HE REALLY WANTS IT, MAYBE HE WILL...
30A
YEAH, WELL, JUST IN CASE... COME HERE, YOU!
THE PEOPLE'S BIRD IS FLYING!
30B

THEY'RE FOLLOWING THE PATH OF THE KLAAR! THE MASTER WILL BE FURIOUS WITH US!

AND ONLY HE KNOWS WHEN WISDOM WILL REACH THEM!

WE MUST CATCH THEM BEFORE THEY REACH THE FORBIDDEN LANDS!

THEY'RE RIGHT BEHIND US!

DON'T YOU WORRY... PPRRR... THEY WON'T FOLLOW US WHERE WE'RE GOING!

STOP THE CHASE!

HERE BEGINS THE MASTER'S PRIVATE DOMAIN!

NO ONE HAS EVER GONE THERE SINCE THE PATHS OF THE KLAAR WERE BUILT!

LET THEM RUSH TO THEIR DOOM, THEN...

AS THE HEAVY CHARIOT PUSHES DEEPER INTO THE MISTS THAT FOREVER COVER THE FORBIDDEN LANDS...

THAT'S IT! WE'RE SAFE NOW...

UH, HUH. YES, ONCE AGAIN YOU CERTAINLY HAD THINGS COMPLETELY UNDER CONTROL THE WHOLE TIME...

SO, CAN YOU TELL ME WHAT WE DO NOW?

WELL...

SILLY QUESTION!... CRRR... WE'RE GONNA DO THE MASTER IN, AREN'T WE, LAURELINE? CHECK IT OUT...

ALL WE HAVE TO DO IS FOLLOW THE KLAAR, AND... CRITCH... WE'LL REACH HIM. THEN... CRUCK... WE'LL BE FREE AND I'LL SEE MANADIL AGAIN.

YOU'RE PROBABLY RIGHT, SÜL. BESIDES, IT'S THE ONLY THING LEFT TO DO...

AH! I KNEW YOU'D HEAR THE CALL OF DUTY AGAIN...

DUTY... PFFT. I'M DOING IT FOR SÜL, NOT FOR DUTY.

DUTY? WHAT'S THAT?... ANOTHER ONE OF THOSE MOLECULE-BUSTING IDEAS, I'M SURE...

I'M TELLING YOU... BLOOK... OUR ONLY DUTY IS PROSPECTING, THAT'S ALL!

OBJECTIVELY SPEAKING, DUTY IS THE EXPRESSION OF SOCIAL FORCES...

I BEG TO... PLUTSH... DIFFER! IT'S A SUBJECTIVE NOTION THAT...

I'M GOING TO FLY... CLICK... A LITTLE FOR THE PEOPLE!

MAYBE WE SHOULD... CRRAAA... CHANGE OUR OUTFITS TO VISIT THIS MASTER...

AND DO SOMETHING FOR OUR ORGANISER. I FIND THAT GIRL SIMPLY TOO UNKEMPT...

TIME PASSES SLOWLY...

STILL FOLLOWING THE PATHS OF THE KLAAR...   ... THE LITTLE GROUP KEEPS HEADING DOWN.

SUDDENLY, WHILE THE CHARIOT IS CROSSING A WIDE PLATEAU COVERED WITH A FOUL-SMELLING FILM OF BRACKISH WATER...

THE BIRDS OF MADNESS!

I'VE NEVER SEEN SO MANY!... CRRR... THE MASTER'S DECIDED TO GET US THIS TIME!!

THERE! POSSIBLE COVER!

THEY'RE ATTACKING!!

WE'RE DONE FOR!

NO! COME ON!

THEN, AMIDST THE BIRDS' SHRIEKS AND BEATING WINGS...

EVERYONE AROUND THEM! HURRY!...

... THE BIRDS OF MADNESS CAN'T DO ANYTHING TO US ANYMORE—WE'RE ALL ALREADY MAD!

LET'S SHIELD THEM!

ME, TOO!... PRRR... HORRIBLE SOUNDS!

AAAAH! I'VE BEEN BIITEN!... CRIIITCH... IT'S LIKE STATIC!

HOLD TIGHT! KEEP FIRING!

35 A

THE BIRDS ARE RETREATING!

ARE YOU... BZZZ... BADLY HIT?

BAH. I'M USED TO IT BY NOW!... CREEE... I FEEL WEIRD, BUT CONSCIOUS...

VERY INTERESTING... PRRRR... THIS CONFIRMS MY THEORY! THOSE BIRDS... OOG... ARE MERE ILLUSIONS.

SEE!... OOOOP... WE CAN BEAT THE MASTER'S STINKING COPS— AND... CLICK... HIM, TOO, FOR SURE!!

AND THESE BODIES? ILLUSIONS AS WELL? NO, THE YOUNG ONE IS... TAK... RIGHT. THEY'RE THE MASTER'S ENFORCERS.

LOOK AT US NOW... CRRR... I'M SICK OF THOSE NASTY BIRDS!

AND I HAVE... BIMP... NOTHING LEFT TO WEAR! THAT HORRIBLE MASTER WILL HEAR ABOUT IT!

HEY! LOOK AT THAT!!

OH, WHAT IS... BIMP... IT THIS TIME?

I'M NOT GOING ANYWHERE... GLUCK... THIS PLACE LOOKS GREAT.

35 B

THIS IS... SCRATCH... A GOOD PLACE TO FLY. SHALL I?!

WHOA! NO CRAZY STUFF... WELL, I MEAN...

HUH?... THERE'S A LIGHT DOWN THERE!?!

AND THERE!! ALL THE PATHS OF THE KLAAR!!!

LET'S GO DOWN!

I'M SURE... IKKK... THAT IT'S THE MASTER!

I'VE GOT NOTHING AGAINST THE MASTER...

ME, NEITHER! ACTUALLY, I'M GOING TO PROSPECT FOR HIM A BIT...

YOU'RE RIGHT! I'LL GIVE YOU A HAND! WE LAZYBONES CAN BUCKLE DOWN LIKE NO ONE ELSE, YOU'LL SEE!...

HUH?... WHAT ABOUT ME, THEN? THE MASTER AIN'T GONNA LOVE ME IF I DON'T DO ANY WORK...

WHAT DID I TELL YOU?... CLOP... THEY WERE HIT BEFORE US. THE VENOM IS STARTING TO TAKE EFFECT...

NONSENSE. IT'S... PROTCH... THE MASTER'S WILL IMPOSING ITSELF LITTLE BY LITTLE!

AT ANY RATE, WE MIGHT AS WELL LEAVE THEM HERE...

WHAT ABOUT US, VALERIAN?... WE'VE ALL BEEN BITTEN NOW!

YES, WE HAVE TO HURRY.

WE'D DAMNED WELL BETTER... BECAUSE I HAVE NO INTENTION... SLUP... OF SPENDING THE REST OF MY YOUTH SLAVING AWAY FOR THE MASTER!...
LET'S GO!

THROUGH A STEADILY THICKENING
ATMOSPHERE...

... A DANGEROUS DESCENT BEGINS...

... A FRIGHTENING DIVE INTO
THE MASTER'S IMPREGNABLE
DOMAIN...

... UNTIL, AT LAST...

THE MASTER!

I CAN'T BELIEVE MY EYES!!

I CAN, OF COURSE... IKKK... BUT WHAT CAN WE DO AGAINST THAT THING?

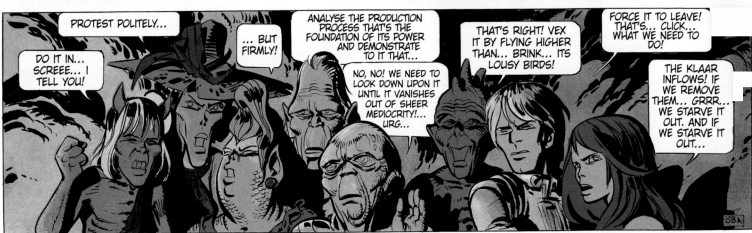

PROTEST POLITELY...

... BUT FIRMLY!

DO IT IN... SCREEE... I TELL YOU!

ANALYSE THE PRODUCTION PROCESS THAT'S THE FOUNDATION OF ITS POWER AND DEMONSTRATE TO IT THAT...

NO, NO! WE NEED TO LOOK DOWN UPON IT UNTIL IT VANISHES OUT OF SHEER MEDIOCRITY!... URG...

THAT'S RIGHT! VEX IT BY FLYING HIGHER THAN... BRINK... ITS LOUSY BIRDS!

FORCE IT TO LEAVE! THAT'S... CLICK... WHAT WE NEED TO DO!

THE KLAAR INFLOWS! IF WE REMOVE THEM... GRRR... WE STARVE IT OUT. AND IF WE STARVE IT OUT...

GOT IT! I'LL GIVE IT A SHOT!... GGLLL... TAKE COVER...

... TAKE OVER IF I FAIL!

ADVANCING SLOWLY ONTO THE OPEN SPACE SURROUNDING THE MASTER...

... ITS MASSIVE, SOFT BODY REACTING WITH NOTHING MORE THAN A SLIGHT QUIVERING...

... VALERIAN OPENS FIRE.

166

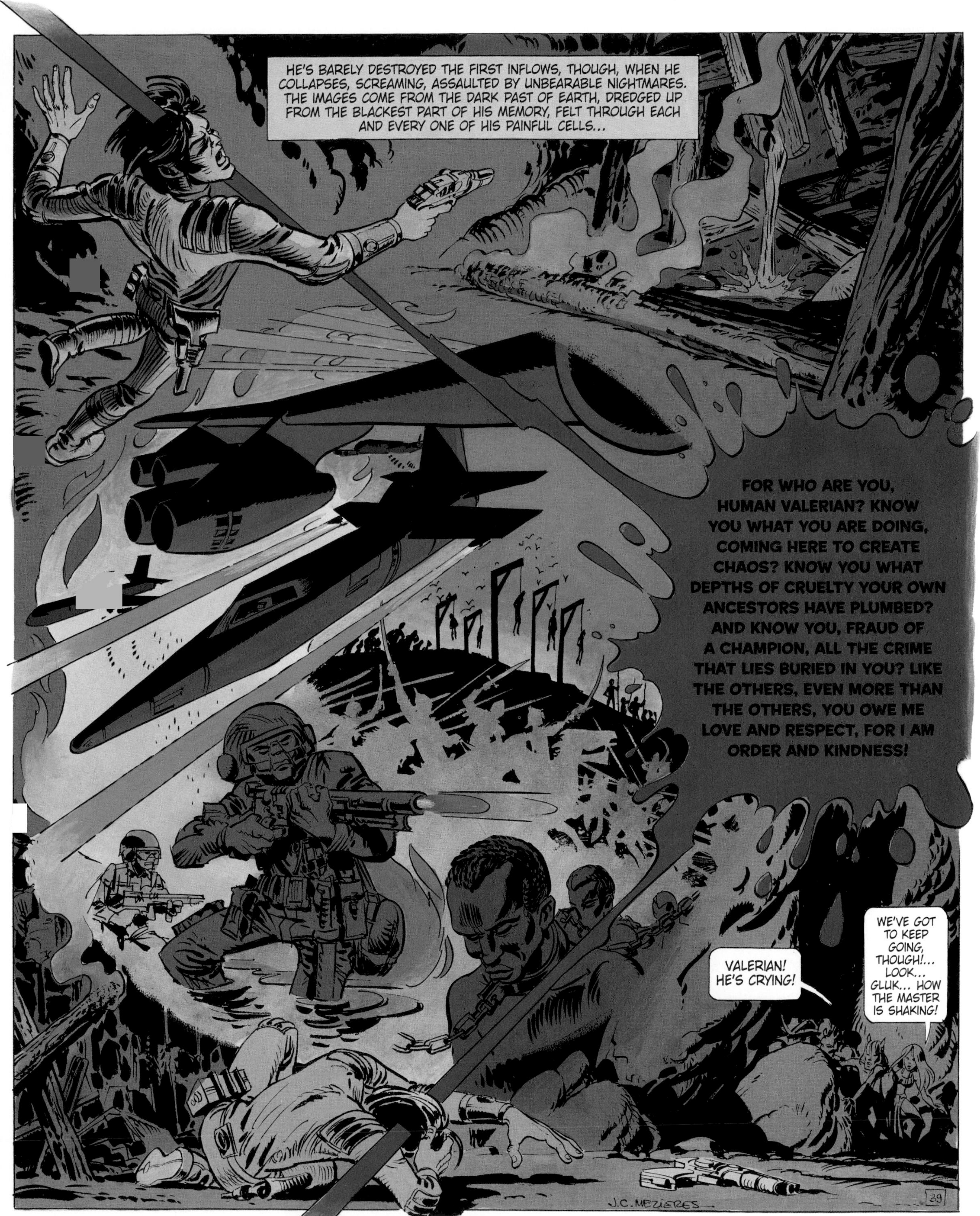
HE'S BARELY DESTROYED THE FIRST INFLOWS, THOUGH, WHEN HE COLLAPSES, SCREAMING, ASSAULTED BY UNBEARABLE NIGHTMARES. THE IMAGES COME FROM THE DARK PAST OF EARTH, DREDGED UP FROM THE BLACKEST PART OF HIS MEMORY, FELT THROUGH EACH AND EVERY ONE OF HIS PAINFUL CELLS...
FOR WHO ARE YOU, HUMAN VALERIAN? KNOW YOU WHAT YOU ARE DOING, COMING HERE TO CREATE CHAOS? KNOW YOU WHAT DEPTHS OF CRUELTY YOUR OWN ANCESTORS HAVE PLUMBED? AND KNOW YOU, FRAUD OF A CHAMPION, ALL THE CRIME THAT LIES BURIED IN YOU? LIKE THE OTHERS, EVEN MORE THAN THE OTHERS, YOU OWE ME LOVE AND RESPECT, FOR I AM ORDER AND KINDNESS!
VALERIAN! HE'S CRYING!
WE'VE GOT TO KEEP GOING, THOUGH!... LOOK... GLUK... HOW THE MASTER IS SHAKING!
J.C. MEZIERES
39

IT'S LAURELINE'S TURN TO LEAP OUT, ONLY TO COLLAPSE SUDDENLY AS WELL, OVERWHELMED BY A THOUSAND EXCRUCIATING VISIONS...

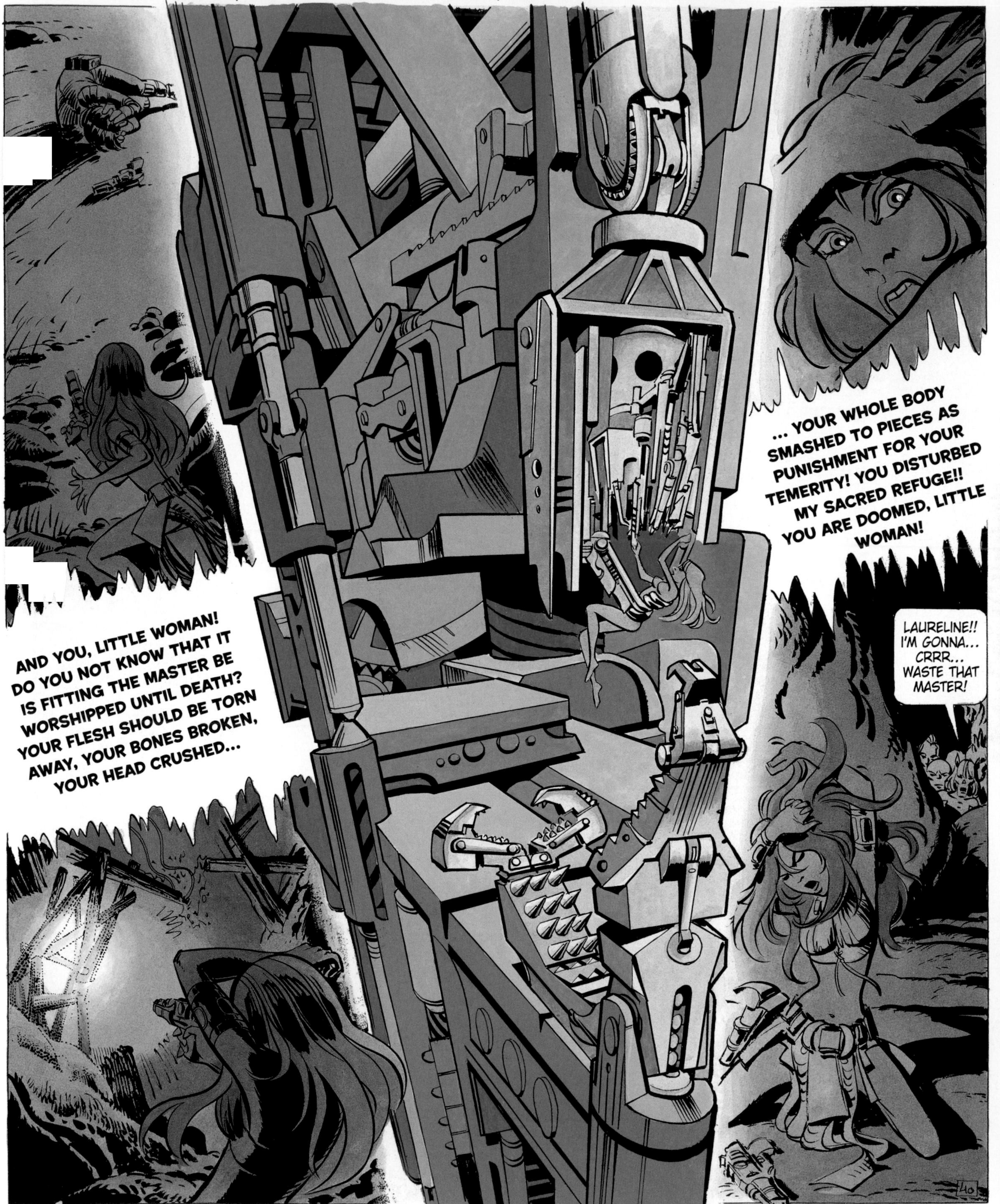

LIKE SÜL, THOUGH, THE MEMBERS OF THE SMALL GROUP COLLAPSE ONE BY ONE. SOON, A SCENE OF UTTER DESOLATION UNFOLDS OVER THE KLAAR SPILLING TO THE GROUND WITH A WARM FRAGRANCE-ANOTHER TORTURE TO THE STARVING BAND-AS ALL OF THEM GIVE IN TO THEIR OWN NIGHTMARES AND TERRORS...

MAN-EATING SPONGES FOR THOSE HAILING FROM DISTANT ERISTRENE...

... FOUL, SLIMY GLATUFILS THAT THE CHILDREN OF RUMUL FEAR SO MUCH...

... VENOMOUS STONES THAT TERRIFY THE INHABITANTS OF ORTOKZOK.

AND YET...

DREAMS—IT'S ALL JUST DREAMS! I... ARRGH... KNOW IT...

WE ARE NOT... CLACK... GOING TO FEEL SORRY FOR OURSELVES!

HEY!... VALERIAN! CAN YOU HEAR ME?

YES... OHHH... URG... MY HEAD!!

THE MASTER... HE'S DESTROYING... GRRNN... US BECAUSE WE'RE ATTACKING HIM SEPARATELY. ALL TOGETHER... LIKE WE DID WITH THE BIRDS... WE CAN WIN...

YES... GET... EVERYONE UP...

HOLD ME TIGHT!

I'M HERE!

TAKE MY HAND!

VALERIAN, HELP ME...

LOOK UPON THE MASTER!

AND SUDDENLY, WITH A GREAT TEARING SOUND...

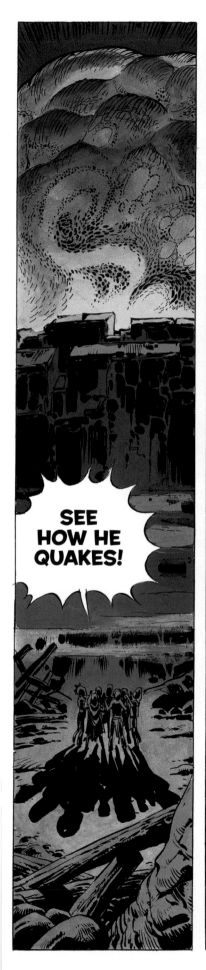

171

NO MORE MASTER!

AH! I'VE BEEN HUNGRY FOR SO LONG. LET'S CELEBRATE!

PURE NECTAR!! YOU KNOW... THIS CRUISE MAKES ME WANT TO...

... STAY HERE, AFTER ALL? THE ATMOSPHERE IS IMPROVING!

MAYBE ONCE I'M WELL FED, I CAN ACTUALLY FLY FOR REAL!

NOT AT ALL! THE BEAUTY OF SEIZING POWER IS THE VICTORY OVER A CLASS ENEMY... 'SCUSE ME, MOVE OVER A BIT...

MMM... THIS LIQUID IS DELICIOUS! IT'S AS IF ALL THAT CAME BEFORE NEVER EXISTED, AS IF ALL WAS HARMONY AND BLISS...

HEY, HOW ABOUT WE REBUILD THE KLAAR INFLOWS AND SETTLE DOWN HERE? WOULDN'T THAT BE AWESOME?

YEAH! ROLL ON THE GOOD TIMES!!!

WHOA... DO YOU HEAR THEM?

ERM! SOME REVOLUTION... I'M NOT IMPRESSED!

THIS SEEMS TO ME LIKE THE PERFECT TIME FOR ONE OF THOSE LITTLE SPEECHES YOU LIKE SO MUCH. ONLY, CONVINCING, THIS TIME... YOU KNOW WHAT I MEAN?

HA, HA. VERY FUNNY!

YOU SHOULD BE ASHAMED OF YOURSELVES, THE LOT OF YOU! THE MASTER'S ONLY BEEN GONE A MINUTE AND ALL YOU THINK ABOUT IS TAKING HIS PLACE! WHAT ABOUT ALL THE POOR BASTARDS BREAKING THEIR BACKS UP THERE TO PREPARE THE KLAAR YOU'RE GULPING DOWN? HAVE YOU THOUGHT ABOUT THEM, HUH?!

HEY, SOUNDS LIKE HE'S BETTER THAN USUAL. IT'S SOLID, SNAPPY... FINALLY.

AND YOU, SÜL? DON'T YOU WANT TO SEE YOUR BEAUTIFUL PLANET AGAIN?

WELL... YEAH...

SO?

YES... WE WERE RATHER SILLY, WEREN'T WE?

ER... MY FEET LEFT THE GROUND FOR A MOMENT...

IT'S JUST THAT WE HAVEN'T HAD MUCH CHANCE TO HAVE FUN UNTIL NOW...

MAYBE WE DID LOSE CONTROL A LITTLE...

THAT KLAAR GOES RIGHT TO YOUR HEAD!

BUT IT'S OVER NOW. WE'RE LEAVING!

LET'S GO, THEN! WE'LL TELL THE MASTER'S CITIES AND LANDS THAT THEY'RE FREE!

I GUESS THIS MISSION IS A COMPLETE AND RESOUNDING SUCCESS, THEN. RIGHT, O MIGHTY LEADER?

45A

LATER, IN THE MIDDLE OF THE STARSHIP CEMETERY...

THAT'S IT! THEY'RE FREE!

45B

173

... THEN, ABOVE THE SMALL PLANETOID STILL LOCKED ON ITS ERRATIC COURSE...

WELL! THE LIFT-OFF WENT MUCH BETTER THAN THE LANDING!

YES. BUT THE SHIP NEEDS A FULL CHECK-UP AS SOON AS WE REACH GALAXITY. HALF THE INSTRUMENTS ARE DEAD.

BETTER MAKE IT QUICK, THEN, BECAUSE I REALLY MISS MANADIL!

... THROUGH THE DARK DEPTHS OF SPACE...

DO YOU THINK THE OTHERS WILL MAKE IT DOWN THERE?

DON'T WORRY, SÜL. SINCE YOU'RE THE ONLY ONE WHO DECIDED TO LEAVE THE MASTER'S FORMER DOMINIONS, YOU'LL SOON BE BACK HOME.

... WHERE ENCOUNTERS WITH UNKNOWN LIFE FORMS STILL FILL MAN WITH TERROR...

HMM... IT WON'T BE EASY FOR THEM TO LEARN TO BE FREE AGAIN. BUT THEY DESTROYED THE KLAAR BASINS AND ARE REORGANISING THEIR PRODUCTION ALONG A COMMUNAL BASIS, SO IT'S OFF TO A GOOD START... IT'LL BE UP TO THEM!

... WHERE THE MYSTERY OF THE UNSPEAKABLE IS STILL PRESENT...

I'M MORE WORRIED ABOUT THE FACT THAT THE MASTER IS SOMEWHERE OUT THERE...

YES. AND, SINCE HIS POWER COMES FROM OTHERS' RESIGNATION, HE WON'T HAVE ANY TROUBLE FINDING PLACES WHERE THEY LIKE AUTHORITY! HE'S A CUNNING ONE, THAT BIG GLUTTON!

... WHERE EVERYTHING IS POSSIBLE, THE SHIP FLIES AWAY...

WELL, LET'S JUST HOPE HE KEEPS TO LESS FREQUENTED AREAS...

SO, ARE WE JUMPING TO YOUR GALAXY OR WHAT?

YES, WE'RE READY.

THE END

SCRIPT: CHRISTIN DRAWING: J.C. MEZIERES 1973

174

VALERIAN

CHRISTIN
MÉZIÈRES
VALERIAN
THE COMPLETE COLLECTION
VOLUME 1
CINEBOOK
The 9th Art Publisher

COMING SOON

CHRISTIN
MÉZIÈRES
VALERIAN
THE COMPLETE COLLECTION
VOLUME 2
CINEBOOK
The 9th Art Publisher

CHRISTIN
MÉZIÈRES
VALERIAN
THE COMPLETE COLLECTION VOLUME 3
CINEBOOK
The 9th Art Publisher

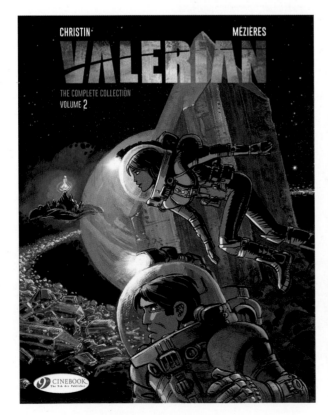

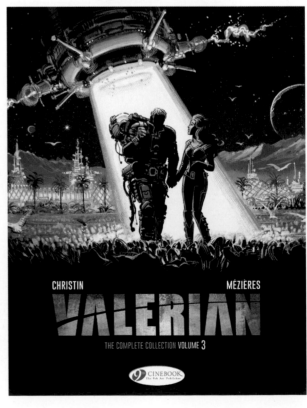